STAR WARS YOGA, THE FORCE, AND YOU
By CARY BAYER

This book is dedicated to:

Val Vadeboncoeur for showing me an Internet link that led me to explore the Anthroposophical influence on George Lucas, which led me step by step to expand a shorter mini-book into this full-length work.

***STAR WARS* YOGA, THE FORCE, & YOU**

© Copyright 2017, by Cary Bayer

No part of this book may be reproduced by any mechanical, photographic, or electronic process, or in the form of a phonographic recording, nor may it be stored in a retrieval system, transmitted, or otherwise be copied for public or private use—other than for "fair use"—without written permission of the publisher.

Heaven on Earth Publishing
Bayer Communications
1051 Hillsboro Mile Apt. 604
Hillsboro Beach, FL 33062

Cover and book design: Jeff Williamson, Avenue C Productions

BY CARY BAYER:

Books

The Prosperity Aerobics
40 Days to a Happy Life
Relationships 101
Conscious Communication
A Course in Money *Miracles*
How to Overcome Procrastination Now
Higher Self Meditations
Breakthrough Coaching
The Yoga of Entertainment: Higher Consciousness in Pop Culture
"Star Wars" Yoga, the Force, & You
Wohlstands Aerobic (German translation of *The Prosperity Aerobics*)
Think and Grow a Rich Massage Business
Market and Grow a Rich Massage Business
Communicate and Grow a Rich Massage Business
Trump Off the Wall (That Mexico's Gonna Pay For)
Spiritual Lampoons
The Short Report: Good News for Guy's 5'7" & Under, with Robert Levine
Fire Island Fried: An Irreverent Guide to an Irreverent Island,
    with Robert Romagnoli

Mini-Books

How to Discover & Live Your Purpose
Spirit & Money
Awaken your Creative Genius
Zen Teachings of Oz
Walt Whitman: Poet of Enlightenment
Healer, Heal Thyself
Literary Yoga: Writers & Higher Consciousness
Follow Your Yellow Brick Road: Provisions for your Inner Journey
Zen Teachings of Animals
Zen Teachings of Cats and Dogs
Zen Teachings of Sports
Zen Teachings of Tennis

Magnetizando el Dinero (Spanish translation of *Magnetizing Money*)
Lampoons for a New Millennium
Zen in the Art of the Marx Brothers
Zen in the Art of Harpo
Laughter is the Jest Medicine: Thoughts to Laugh By

TABLE OF CONTENTS

CHAPTER		PAGE
	Preface to the Prequels / The *Star Wars* Lineup	9-10
	Introduction	11
1.	*Star Wars*, the Force, & You	15
2.	*Star Wars* Yoga: Contacting the Force Through Meditation	23
3.	Life When the Force is With You	29
4.	Yoda Yoga	33
5.	The Buddha & Yoda	41
6.	The Force & the Tao	47
7.	Skywalkers & Desert Walkers: Judaism & Jediism	51
8.	The Gospel of Luke (Skywalker): Jesus & the Jedis	55
9.	Satan & the Dark Side of the Force	61
10.	Jedi Knights & the Round Table: *Star Wars*, Camelot, & the Middle Ages	65
11.	A New Mythos from a Galaxy Far, Far Away	69
12.	The Dark Side & the Shadow: Jung at Heart	75
13.	*Star Wars* & *Star Trek*	79
14.	Superman, Wolverine, & Yoda: Jedi Knights as Superheroes	83
15.	How Anthroposophy Resuscitated a Dying *Star Wars* Script	89
16.	Luke's Unconsciousness of His Family: A Metaphor for Reconnecting to Your Source	95
17.	Sayings from a Galaxy Far, Far Away	99
18.	Introduction: Affirming your Call to the Adventure of Peaceful Jedi Mind Training	109
19.	Jedi Mind Training: Affirmations for Aligning with the Force	113
20.	Epilogue: Final Thoughts From A Galaxy Close, Close to You	137
	About the Author	141
	Additional Reading	142
	Calling all Producers: Cary Bayer's Intro & Full-Day Workshops	145
	Growth Products from Cary Bayer	148

"May the Force be with you."
— *Star Wars* mantra

"The conclusion I've come to is that all the religions are true."
— George Lucas

PREFACE TO THE PREQUELS

Let me start off the bat by saying unequivocally that I am not a *Star Wars* freak or geek. I don't own a single *Star Wars* T-shirt, I have none of the videos of any of the films in the series, and I have never gone to Comic Con International in San Diego where, every summer, hundreds of superhero fans and *Star Wars* geeks attend (often in elaborate costume). All I own in the way of *Star Wars* merchandise is a Yoda mouse pad, statue, and live action figure.

So why, you might ask, did I write this book in the first place? The reason, as you'll soon see in the Introduction that follows, is that the George Lucas sci-fi saga—or space opera, if you prefer—is rich in spiritual truths. For those of you whose consciousness is far, far away from the enormous phenomenon that is *Star Wars*, the pop culture extravaganza that is *Star Wars* began in 1977 with the launch of the first of eight films. For those who lack the ability to cite each film in its place in the series, here's a scorecard to tell the players.

THE *STAR WARS* LINEUP

1977 *Star Wars*, the fourth film in the series. (A prequel trilogy followed the original trilogy). This film is now designated as number IV in the series, even though it hit the world's cineplexes years before any of the others—and 22 years before the movie now designated as I. Now that we got that piece of confusion out of the way.

1980	*The Empire Strikes Back*	(V)
1983	*Return of the Jedi*	(VI)
1999	*The Phantom Menace*	(I)
2002	*Attack of the Clones*	(II)
2005	*Revenge of the Sith*	(III)
2015	*The Force Awakens*	(VII)
2016	*Rogue One: A "Star Wars" Story*	(VIII)
2017	*Star Wars: The Last Jedi*	(Tentatively December 15)
2018	*Untitled Han Solo Movie*	(Tentatively May 25)
2019	*Star Wars: Episode IX,*	(Tentatively May 24)

INTRODUCTION

On June 22, 2016, on the anniversary of the birthday of my late father, who fortunately never did succumb to the dark side of the Force, I presented, for the first time, my workshop, "*Star Wars* Yoga, the Force, & You," at a wonderful metaphysical center in Hollywood, Florida called Crystal Vision. A few days afterwards, I was inspired to create a 48-page mini-book called *"Star Wars" Jedi Mind Training: Affirmations for Aligning with the Force*, so that those in attendance in future classes might have something of a *Star Wars* nature to take home with them after they have left the class and driven away in their cars, hopefully not at warp speed—although, disappearing into hyperspace is one darned good way to confound police radar guns and beat traffic every time.

On July 12, my longtime buddy Val Vadeboncoeur, an ardent admirer of Rudolph Steiner and his Anthroposophy metaphysical system, sent me an email inviting me to check out an Internet link to an article about the role that Anthroposophy played in inspiring a creatively blocked George Lucas and his film editor wife Marcia to transform their stuck second draft of *Star Wars*. Had the events depicted in that article not occurred there might never have been an original *Star Wars* film, to say nothing of an eleven-part sci-fi saga, an intergalactic new mythos, or a spaceship full of money for George Lucas. And certainly no 2012 sale of his Lucasfilm to the Walt Disney Company for $4,006,000,000. (That's four billion, six million dollars for those who don't dabble in that many zeroes.)

I was so busy that 11 days and 11 nights passed before I had a moment to read the rather long Internet piece that Val had sensed I would enjoy. By the time I had finished the article, I had decided to re-tell the story and add it to my mini-book. But then, I thought: what about the well-known Joseph Campbell influence on Lucas, which I taught about in my workshop? Shouldn't I say something about that in the mini-book? And ditto the Yoda Yoga influence, also a rich part of my class? As my workshop teaches, *Star Wars* contains elements of the Perennial Philosophy, Aldous Huxley's term from his eponymous book to denote the one wisdom that has appeared in diverse forms as religions, philosophical and metaphysical systems, and so forth throughout time and space. (That's space as in different areas of the globe, not outer space. Cancel clear: delete the previous sentence from your understanding; after all, this is a book about *Star Wars*.)

One Internet link linked me to yet another. Within days I had decided to expand the 48-page photocopied and stapled mini-book, which was a series of affirmations to align with the Force, to this full-length bound book you're holding now. Soon thereafter, I would Google books written about the spirituality of *Star Wars*. (See Additional Reading at the end of this volume.)

I created my workshop in the first place to teach the timeless wisdom of Yoga, myth, and Jungian insights in the context of the contemporary mega-phenomena called *Star Wars*. Now, about a year after reading that Internet piece, I'm writing this introduction to a book that significantly expanded upon the material in that class.

There's the rich Yogic spirituality (chapter 4), the wisdom of the Tao (chapter 6), Buddha's teaching (chapter 5), the Jews and the Jedis (chapter 7), the Luke of *Star Wars* and the Luke of the Gospels (chapter 8), rich Jungian insights (chapter 12), the Jedi knights and the knights of the Round Table (chapter 10), the treasure trove of mythic import (chapter 11), modern day comic book superheroes and the super powers of the Jedis (chapter 14), and the Anthroposophy wisdom (chapter 15), without which there might never have been a *Star Wars* film produced as we know it.

There are also chapters devoted to understanding the relationships between the Force and yourself (chapter 1), how to contact the Force through meditation (chapter 2), the benefits of living life in tune with the Force (chapter 3), the dangers of living in the dark side of the Force and Satan (chapter 9), and the relationship of the dark side to your Shadow, as depicted by C.G. Jung (chapter 12). You'll also get a warp speed look at the relationship between *Star Wars* and *Star Trek* (chapter 13). What's more, you'll see how Luke Skywalker's unconsciousness of his family of origin is a metaphor for disconnection from your Source, and how it invites you to consciously connect to It (chapter 16). Finally, you'll read some of the wisest sayings from this magnificent science fiction space opera (chapter 17), learn how to align with the Force through affirmation (chapter 18), and discover many dozens of such affirmations that can help you do just that (chapter 19).

Most of all, you'll come away with an even finer appreciation with the saga that is *Star Wars*, so that when you see the films that have not yet been released, or when you revisit the ones that have, you'll see a rich mythology and spirituality that gives a depth to the characters on the screen. I hope you enjoy all of that wisdom so that it may help align you with the Force that is your Source.

— Cary Bayer
August 2017
Woodstock, NY

"Always remember, your focus determines your reality."

— George Lucas

CHAPTER 1
STAR WARS, THE FORCE, & YOU

I along with most everyone else in America, have seen *Star Wars: The Force Awakens*, the most current installment of the *Star Wars* franchise. George Lucas films have much to teach us spiritually. And financially, as well, as its most recent entry has become the highest grossing film of all time in America, and is well on its way to being the highest grossing film worldwide, as well. Which is a good thing that the two highest grossing films ever—it and *Avatar*—both have deeply important spiritual lessons to impart to moviegoers. (I devoted an entire chapter to *Avatar* in my previous book, *The Yoga of Entertainment: Higher Consciousness in Pop Culture*, in 2016.)

It's hard to get a clear handle on just how enormously successful the franchise is, but estimates from the end of 2015 have it in excess of $33.5 billion, an intergalactic level of success if ever there was one. Box office revenues for the first seven released films are in the vicinity of $13.5 billion. Interestingly, Lucas was paid a relatively meager $150,000 to write and direct the first film. To his negotiating credit— perhaps some connection to the light side of the Force—his company also was guaranteed 40 percent of the movie's net profits. Toys and merchandise totals exceed $12.1 billion, DVD and VHS rentals were some $7.7 billion, video game revenues surpassed $3.4 billion, books totaled more than $1.8 billion, with miscellaneous items approaching $1.9 billion. How would you like to have even a small piece of that miscellany?

The *Star Wars* saga isn't just a mega industry at bijous around the world; it's also something of a movement, perhaps even a religious one. In England and Wales, for example, more than 390,000 citizens listed their religion as Jedi in their 2001 census. In census polls also taken during that year, in excess of 70,000 Aussies did the same; 53,000 folks in New Zealand did, as well; and ditto for 21,000 Canadians and 14,000 Scots. In fact, New Zealanders who called themselves Jedis outnumbered Kiwis who called themselves Buddhists. It seems as if the British Empire is growing its own Jedi empire.

The phenomena, however, wasn't restricted to only English-speaking countries. More than 15,000 people in the Czech Republic declared themselves to be Jedi Knights in their 2001 census. In 2015, more than 6,000 signatures were affixed to a petition in Turkey on change.org saying, "To recruit new Jedi and to bring balance to the Force, we want a Jedi temple." Three years earlier, 640 people in Serbia claimed to be Jedis. The year before that, 303 citizens in Croatia did the same. That same year, an unnamed number of people in Montenegro followed suit on their census forms. In 1986, President Reagan boasted that, "the Force is with us," a most decidedly pop culture manner of expression to echo Bob Dylan's song, "With God on our Side." At the turn of the new millennium, the American Film Institute ranked the top 100 movie quotes of all time and placed, "May the Force be with you," at number 8. A decade and a half later, the Force is still a force in our culture: a highway billboard from Xfinity reads: "The Force is strong with this one."

Journalist Bill Moyers shared an experience that he had with his son that echoes this Jedi religious phenomenon. When the newsman asked his son why he had seen *Star Wars* more than a dozen times, the boy responded, "For the same reason you have been reading the *Old Testament* all your life." Moyers' response was terse; he knew that he was in "a new world of myth."

For a measly $8.99, anyone can purchase a Jedi Knight Certificate from Universal Life Church Monastery, which depicts itself as "one of Earth's newest religions," on the website, (https://www.themonastery.org/catalog/jediknightcertificate-p-237.html) If that's not enough, you can also become a Jedi minister (http://ordainme.weebly.com/jedi.html) and get a Jedi marriage certificate at http://www.jedichurch.org/jedi-marriage-licence.html.

That new mythos that Moyers referred to was on display in a huge "*Star Wars*: The Magic of Myth" exhibit at the National Air and Space Museum of the Smithsonian Institution that ran from October 1997 through the end of January 1999. The exhibit incorporated the Zoroastrian dualism of good and evil, as well as the concept of the Force, which takes its influence from Eastern philosophies such as Yoga, Buddhism, and Taoism as we'll see in chapters 4, 5, and 6, respectively.

Lucas confided to Moyers in an interview for *Time* magazine: "I see *Star Wars* as taking all the issues that religion represents and trying to distill them down into a more easily accessible construct—that there is a greater mystery out there."

THE FORCE

"May the Force be with you," the saga reminds us repeatedly, acting as a kind of intergalactic cinematic mantra. The irony, however, is that the Force actually always *is* with you. It's only your unconscious thoughts, speech, and actions that make it appear to you as if you're disconnected from It. Since the Force pervades your being, not having It be with you is much like a fish not having water be with it. Not only does the Force pervade your being; in truth it *is* your being, but that insight dawns only in the highest state of consciousness. When you live consciously connected to the Force, your life flows much like a river, and the Universe works to fulfill your desires. As one of Luke's teachers—Obi-Wan Kenobi—told him, "The Force obeys your commands."

We don't know for certain exactly how Lucas came up with the term the Force. We do know, for example, that he had read Carlos Castaneda's *Tales of Power*, where the anthropology student's Yacqui master Don Juan spoke of a "life force." The old shaman was said to be childlike not unlike Yoda, who would play such a huge role in the *Star Wars* series. The vision quest so central to shamanism may have been an influence in Luke's Jedi training under Yoda. When the former descended into a mystical tree, a shamanic-like test if ever there was one, Yoda told his youthful disciple that he may only bring back from the journey whatever he took with him. Namely himself.

What is this Force that Lucas presents? To Obi-Wan, "It surrounds us and penetrates us. It binds the galaxy together." Like the Tao, which is an interpenetration of light and dark forces, it has a light side and a dark. To Lucas himself it's "a nothingness that can accomplish miracles." He went on to elaborate: "Ultimately the Force is the larger mystery of the universe. And to trust your feelings is your way into that."

While Christian influences are absent in *Star Wars*, that hasn't stopped its theologians from seeing the teachings of Christ in the space epic. In a blog called "The Mythology of Star Wars: The Faith versus the Force," (http://www.albertmohler.com/2005/05/25/the-mythology-of-star-wars-the-faith-versus-the-force-2/), Albert Mohler quoted Robert Jewett of Garrett-Evangelical Theological Seminary in Evanston, Illinois, who saw "a compelling gospel in this film, one that deserves to be compared with Paul's words in Romans." Robert E.A. Lee, a Lutheran, said that the Force is an amalgam of "the mysticism of ESP and the New Testament doctrine of the Holy Spirit." Surprisingly, in this blog, neither of these men of the cloth compared a statement by Obi-Wan Kenobi that's an obvious echo of something Jesus said. The latter brought succor to his disciples by saying "And remember, I am with you always, to the end of the age." (Matthew 28:20). The disembodied former Jedi master told Luke: "Remember, the Force will be with you always." And Bryan Stone, author of *Faith and the Film: Theological Themes at the Cinema*, was quoted by John McDowell in the blog, "'Feeling the Force'—Star Wars and Spiritual Truth," (http://www.bethinking.org/culture/feeling-the-force-star-wars-and-spiritual-truth) as saying, "Clearly, the Holy Spirit does bear some resemblance to the Force of *Star Wars*."

Yoda taught Luke that he'd know the difference between the light and the dark sides of the Force when he was "calm, at peace." Luke's father, Anakin, was taught something similar in his Jedi training, when he was told that he would be able to hear the voice of the midi-chlorians, which help human beings understand the Force. "When you learn to quiet your mind," the master told the young Skywalker, "you will hear them speaking to you."

Tantric Yoga, an ancient practice that involves transformation through a number of methods including the sex act, also has a light side and a dark side as part of its esoteric teachings. The same can be said of magic: there's white magic as well as its black counterpart. Yoda spelled out in a very clear way the power that comes with adherence to the light side of the Force while teaching Luke, his young charge:

> "For my ally is the Force. And a powerful ally it is. Life creates it, makes it grow. Its energy surrounds us and binds us…You must feel the Force around you. Here, between you…me…the tree…the rock…everywhere! Yes, even between the land and the ship!"

The Force, we're told, was tapped through one's sensitivity to the midi-chlorians. These microscopic intelligent life forms exist within the cells of all living beings, Qui-Gon Jinn taught Anakin Skywalker as part of his Jedi training. The master imparted the following to his student:

> *"Without the midi-chlorians, life could not exist, and we would have no knowledge of the Force. They continually speak to us, telling us the will of the Force. When you learn to quiet your mind, you'll hear them speaking to you."*

Jedis could determine how much of the Force was manifest in a person simply by examining his midi-chlorian count. This could be determined by analyzing one's blood. Anakin Skywalker registered the highest midi-chlorian count ever recorded—in excess of 20,000—a quantitative reason why he was thought to be the Chosen One who was prophesized to the Jedis. The midi-chlorians were believed to play a role in the development of eternal consciousness. This helps to explain how Obi-Wan Kenobi, for example, was able to communicate in a disembodied form to Luke even after his death.

The Force was particularly lively in certain locations, such as the Dagobah cave where Luke received his Jedi training. A pair of planets—Mortis and Moraband—were also said to be rich in the Force.

Yoda said of the Force's dark side: "Fear is the path to the dark side. Fear leads to anger, anger leads to hate, hate leads to suffering." This is the temptation that Luke's father Anakin succumbed to. It's a temptation that some yogis have also succumbed to. It's a temptation that Tantrics have succumbed to. And it's a temptation that magicians have succumbed to. It's a temptation that Satan tried to get Jesus to succumb to. And it's a temptation that Mara tried to get the Buddha to succumb to before he became the Buddha; he became the Awakened One, in part, because he resisted that temptation. In Episode 5 of the *Star Wars* saga (*The Empire Strikes Back*) Yoda told Luke that, "Once you start down the path of the dark side, forever will it dominate your destiny."

Like the story told in India's *Bhagavad Gita*, the textbook of Yoga, Lucas has spun a cinematic tale that's intended to be one part political, one part military, and one part spiritual. In fact, the director said he read some 50 books on religion in preparation for creating his saga. The author who most influenced him was the great mythologist Joseph Campbell; the book that most influenced the filmmaker was the professor's *A Hero with a Thousand Faces*. As Lucas said, "The stories I found most interesting are stories of Zen education or the Zen master teaching a pupil how to transcend physical prowess into some kind of mental process. That's what all the training sequences are about."

In schooling Lucas in preparation of his script, Campbell told him stories from the great Indian epics, *The Mahabharata* (from which the

Bhagavad Gita is included) and *The Ramayana*, in particular. At a tribute to Campbell, Lucas called the mythologist, "my Yoda." As you'll see in chapter 15, Anthroposophy also played a major role in the shaping of the original film in the series.

An unnamed blogger, writing in a piece called "Yoda and Yoga," on belief.net (http://www.beliefnet.com/entertainment/movies/2005/05/yoda-and-yoga.aspx?), cited this tale:

> "A beautiful princess is kidnapped by a powerful but evil warlord. With determined urgency, a mysterious non-human entity delivers a distress call to a budding young hero. The youthful hero, a prince, comes to the princess's rescue, aided by a noble creature that is half-man and half-animal. In the end, after a war that epitomizes the perennial battle between good and evil, the beautiful maiden returns home. The valiant efforts of the prince and his comrade, who were assisted by an army of anthropomorphic bears in the fight to return the princess to safety, are duly rewarded, and peace and righteousness once again engulf the kingdom."

And no, the story above is not from a galaxy far, far away, but from our own; in particular from a part of it called India. Sita is the princess in this legend, the beloved of the god Rama (an incarnation of the god Vishnu, who maintains the Universe), and her captor is the power-hungry Ravana; the story is found in the epic *Ramayana*. Our modern sci-fi fairy tale from a galaxy far, far away echoes this ancient scripture from a time far, far away. We have princesses (Sita and Leia); we have power cravers (Ravana and Darth Vader); we have non-humans who have knowledge of the abduction (a talking bird akin to our vulture named Jatayu, and R2-D2, the android whose memory holds the holographic message left by Leia). We also have a hero (Rama) or one who will become one (Luke Skywalker) who goes to rescue the abducted princess. The heroes are aided by a man/animal (the monkey god Hanuman, and Han Solo and the half-man/half-monkey Wookie Chewbacca). Both stories also feature bloody wars in which good triumphs over evil, the princess is rescued, and harmony prevails in the land once again.

So the next time that you see one of the *Star Wars* films—whether it's the one that has not yet been released or one of the eight that have—realize that many of the same principles of your own spiritual evolution are being depicted right there in 3-D on that movie screen that has so captivated your attention. What was previously popcorn-munching entertainment filled with thrills becomes a kind of enlightenment that might send chills up your spine.

"Just as you wouldn't leave the house without taking a shower, you shouldn't start the day without at least 10 minutes of sacred practice: prayer, meditation, inspirational reading."

— Marianne Williamson

CHAPTER 2
STAR WARS YOGA: CONTACTING THE FORCE THROUGH MEDITATION

As Yoda explained in the previous chapter, the Force "surrounds us and penetrates us." Another way of saying it is that the Force is omnipresent, therefore within us. Such a description makes it sound quite similar to what we in the West call God, (chapters 7 and 8), what the Chinese have called the Tao (chapter 6), and what those in India have called Brahman (chapter 4).

In India, people have contacted Brahman and have come to live in harmony and conscious connection with It through the spiritual disciplines of Yoga and meditation. Having practiced Yoga and meditation since the age of 17, I have seen first hand how powerful and effective the latter is as a tool to expand consciousness and connect the meditator to his or her Source. In India, that source is known as one's higher Self, inner Being, or the Transcendent. The meditation that I practiced from my teen years and taught for more than 30 years, until 2010, was Maharishi Mahesh Yogi's Transcendental Meditation (TM). Since then, I founded Higher Self Healing Meditation, a technique similar to TM, that I developed as a way to make an effortless style of mantra meditation more affordable for the average person than the enormous fees that the TM organization has historically charged.

Yoda told Luke that he would know the Force when his mind was calm and at peace. Qui-Gon Jinn told Anakin that "when you learn to quiet your mind, you will hear them (the midi-chlorians) speak to you." Obi-Wan Kenobi told Luke to "let go of thoughts to hear the Force." Meditation effectively quiets the mind and relaxes the body so that one can truly be deeply calm and at peace, and beyond thoughts in the transcendental part of the mind, which is beyond all activity mental and physical.

Physiological research on Transcendental Meditation, for example, has shown that the technique produces a level of rest that's qualitatively twice as deep as the deepest point in a night's sleep (as measured by oxygen consumption), while the mind is even more alert than it is in normal wakefulness, as measured by EEG equipment. This deep restful alertness has been called a fourth state of consciousness, as distinct from waking, dreaming, and deep sleep as each of these changing states are from one another. I use the word "changing" deliberately because this fourth state of awareness is a non-changing one.

We never see Luke meditating per se in his Jedi training, but we do know that Yoda gave him much to work on in an inner manner. Whether Luke meditated or not, we don't know, but meditation can be used by any one, whether he's a fan of *Star Wars* or not, to contact the inner spirit that Yoda called the Force. What's so interesting about both Transcendental Meditation and Higher Self Healing Meditation, techniques that I've taught to so many hundreds of people, is that both are practiced in an absolutely effortless manner. In other words, no concentration or control of the mind is used; there is no individual effort employed to direct the outcome of the experience. So what makes these methods so effective if it's not the efforts of the practitioners?

To understand this we need to understand two major phenomena in our lives that we notice every single day. The first is the transitions between the changing states of waking, dreaming, and deep sleep. The second is what motivates the mind itself. Let's examine these one at a time.

EFFORTLESS TRANSITIONS

When you go to sleep at night, you set up an initial condition, consisting of turning off the light, putting your head on a pillow, and laying prone on a bed. No amount of trying will enable you to fall asleep more quickly; in fact, any amount of trying will only keep you awake longer. In other words, *trying* to fall asleep is actually counterproductive. It is simply not within your ability to speed up the process of going from waking to sleeping. That's because falling asleep is the domain of another force, a higher power. It's the same force that takes care of beating the heart in your chest, breathing air through your lungs, digesting the foods that you eat and beverages that you drink, and circulating its nutrients throughout your bloodstream. That power goes by many names, but in a galaxy far, far away it's called the Force.

The Force also shifts you from sleeping to dreaming, and, if you don't use an alarm clock, a smart phone, a significant other, a child, a grandchild, a dog, a cat, or a rooster to get you up, you'll get up naturally. In other words, Nature will get you up. And Nature, in fact, is another name for the Force. Maharishi also called this Force the Force of Evolution. Part of Its work involves effortlessly shifting us from one state of consciousness to another for the purpose of purifying our nervous system (waking to sleep) and expanding our aliveness (waking to the transcendental state). It also works to evolve us in a myriad of ways.

THE MOTIVATION OF HAPPINESS

The good news is that, at the depths of the mind of Luke Skywalker, you, and me, is a field of deep peace, calmness, and happiness. Happiness is the operative word here. Luke's mind, your mind, and my mind all gravitate toward happiness. The Force (in Yoda's terminology) or the Force of Evolution (in Maharishi's) is what attracts the mind to greater happiness, to higher states of consciousness, which is what spiritual evolution is all about. I remember one day some years back in my home in Woodstock, New York when I was delivering a talk on Transcendental Meditation I was standing in my living room, in front of sliding glass doors, which looked out onto a deck; beyond that deck was a backyard area and, beyond that, the woods. As I explained to the people who were sitting in front of me, facing outside, the nature of every mind is to experience greater happiness. Moreover, every mind will move to greater happiness, if given the chance, without any effort whatsoever. Just as I said that, several of the people who were seated on the couch and chairs around me suddenly got up from their seats to look behind me. So I turned around, too, curious to see what they were looking at. A mother deer and her baby fawns had just emerged from the depths of the woods and were gamboling across the field. No effort was needed for these people to switch their attention from listening to me talking about the nature of the mind to spontaneously shift to greater happiness, to watching these deer. And the reason, of course, is because watching deer is more enjoyable than listening to a lecture.

Both of the meditation techniques that I have taught for many years give the minds of the many hundreds of people who I taught the opportunity to move towards the greater happiness that exists at the depths of their minds, in the transcendent area beyond change. You don't need to believe in gravity to fall into a swimming pool if you lean in far enough. You don't have to be British like Sir Isaac Newton who formulated the Law of Gravitation, and you don't have to be from India like the yogis who brought effortless meditation into the world, to experience the happiness deep within your mind if you practice Transcendental Meditation or Higher Self Healing Meditation. What you do need, though, is a mantra that best suits your nervous system, and then the effortless manner of using it so that the Force can move your consciousness from waking to the fourth state of consciousness known as pure consciousness or Transcendental Consciousness.

The Force is always moving you toward greater happiness, towards the expanded consciousness of the fourth state, and to the enlightened state of Self-Realization, the fifth state of human consciousness.

"Knowing others is wisdom, knowing yourself is Enlightenment."

— Lao Tzu

CHAPTER 3
LIFE WHEN THE FORCE IS WITH YOU

The most well known and most used expression in the first *Star Wars* motion picture released was "May the Force be with you." In this book I am also equating the Force with your Source, so having It be with you consciously means living a life that is much more abundant and at peace than you would live without conscious connection to the Force. Those in spiritual traditions refer to a life connected to Source as Enlightenment or liberation.

In India, Enlightenment is known, in Sanskrit terms, as Sat Chit Ananda, or Reality, Consciousness, Bliss. Living in such a light means a person has shifted his identification from a limited ego encased in a bag of flesh to the unlimited, unbounded Self outside of time in the Transcendent, that's not contained between one's hat and boots, as Walt Whitman wrote in his epic poem, "Song of Myself."

When a person has become attuned to his higher Self, he no longer lives separately from Nature, but is transformed into a most natural person, one through whom the Intelligence of the Universe expresses itself without a shred of interference from the individual. When you begin the practice of either of the meditation techniques that I've taught and wrote about in the preceding chapter, you begin to rapidly evolve your consciousness. This gives you momentary experiences of the Force. As a result of this, you have the advantage of the Force being more and more with you, so that delightful synchronicities turn out in your favor. The person who has gained Enlightenment on a permanent, around-the-clock basis lives directly from the Force. This 24/7 awareness is a fifth state of consciousness, known in many traditions as Self-Realization. In the seventh state of awareness—Unity Consciousness—one has completely identified oneself with the Force itself. In much the same way that Jesus said, "I and the Father are one," an enlightened Jedi, who has risen to this seventh state of consciousness, might say, "The Force and I are one."

"The person who has gained Enlightenment on a permanent, around-the-clock basis lives directly from the Force."

"Luminous beings we are...not this crude matter."

— Yoda

CHAPTER 4
YODA YOGA

The 11-part franchise—only eight films—have so far been released—has featured one of my all-time favorite spiritual cinema characters—namely, Yoda. This adorable three-foot gnome-like lookalike could easily have been called Yoga, as he taught Luke Skywalker many deeply esoteric things about consciousness and its latent abilities that echo some of the most profound spiritual teachings in the Yoga tradition. You may recall that the pint-sized guru was in excess of 900 years old, reminiscent of the great yogi Babaji, who, followers say, is twice that age, or more than 1,800 years old, and still living in seclusion in the most remote parts of India.

WHAT IS YOGA?

While most of the world thinks of Yoga as a series of stretching poses on a mat in a class for an hour or so, the truth is that it's so much more than that. The word yoga is Sanskrit for yoke or union; specifically the uniting of your individual mind with the Universal Consciousness deep within. Meditation, rather than Hatha Yoga poses (or asanas as they're called in Sanskrit), is a far more effective method for bringing consciousness from the surface of the mind to its transcendental depths, where that Universal Mind happens to be located.

Luke wanted Yoda to teach him to be a Jedi, a kind of spiritual protector of righteousness in the galaxy. In *The Empire Strikes Back*, Yoda explained this role even more clearly: "A Jedi uses the Force for knowledge and defense, never for attack." So, while a Jedi is trained in the arts of war, he does so through the growth of inner peace. His military skills are always intended for defense, and never for offense. A Jedi is quite similar to a yogi, as we'll soon see later in this chapter, when we compare Yoda and Luke of *Star Wars* to Krishna and Arjuna in the *Bhagavad Gita*.

When Luke met Yoda, he told the ancient sage that he was ready to begin his Jedi training. Yoda, however, didn't see that readiness at all, and told the aspirant in *The Empire Strikes Back*:

> "*Ready are you? What know you of ready? For 800 years have I trained Jedi. My own counsel will I keep on who is to be trained. A Jedi must have the deepest commitment, the most serious mind.*"

To a disembodied Obi-Wan Kenobi, who Yoda had trained and who asked the Master to train young Luke, the diminutive sage explained further about the young man's lack of readiness:

> "*This one (Luke) a long time have I watched. All his life he has looked away... to the future, to the horizon. Never his mind on where he was. Hmm? What he was doing. Hmph. Adventure. Heh. Excitement. Heh. A Jedi craves not these things. You are reckless.*"
> —*The Empire Strikes Back*

In time, however, the old master would take on the young student, and begin the inner and outer training that would transform his young disciple into the Jedi hero he would become. Yoda had always been very discerning as to who is to be trained as a Jedi and who is to do the training. A generation prior to the encounter above, the Jedi master was adamant about who was not to conduct the training of Luke's father, the wunderkind Anakin Skywalker.

The Jedi Council taught Qui-Gon Jinn an important lesson of non-attachment, a lesson that all Jedi masters taught to their students, as Yoda taught Luke. Qui-Gon was deeply attached to training Luke's father Anakin, who he scouted as the possible one who prophesy said would unite the Force, but the council nixed the idea unequivocally.

Yoda, who was sitting on the council at the time, said in a coherent, untypically Yoda-like syntax to Qui-Gon Jinn: "Young Skywalker's fate will be decided later."

Qui-Gon, attached to a different result, had a much different idea in mind: "I brought Anakin here; he must stay in my charge. He has nowhere else to go."

Council member Mace Windu responded: "He is your ward, Qui-Gon...we will not dispute that."

Yoda, however, was most definitive: "Train him not. Take him with you, but train him not."

Qui-Gon was taught the lesson of letting go, of not being attached to doing the training. It's a lesson that Obi-Wan, a onetime student of Qui-Gon, would later teach Luke Skywalker, the son of Anakin, when he said, "Let go, Luke."

Arjuna, the military general hero of the *Bhagavad Gita*, was taught a similar lesson as both Luke and Qui-Gon with regard to letting go of attachment to the fruits of action. In verse 45 of the second chapter of the *Gita*, Krishna taught Arjuna to let go of everything he knew when he said, "Be without the three gunas." The gunas are said to be the impulses of Almighty Nature. In other words, the divine teacher advised his human pupil to simply Be.

Qui-Gon brought young Anakin Skywalker in for Jedi training, assuming that he would lead said training. Krishna taught Arjuna a powerful lesson in non-attachment to results, the same lesson that Yoda taught Qui-Gon. Arjuna, however, handled it better than the Jedi when Krishna explained to him:

> *"You have control over action alone, never over its fruits. Live not for the fruits of action, nor attach yourself to inaction."*
> —Chapter 2, verse 47
> All translations are by Maharishi Mahesh Yogi

Cosmic Intelligence takes responsibility for delivering the fruits of action, according to one's karma, Arjuna would learn from his master. In *Star Wars* language, the Force directs that function, and there's nothing a human being—not even a Jedi master—can do about changing that fact of life.

In a previous chapter, we looked at a story from *The Ramayana* of India, which is remarkably similar to the plot line of *Star Wars*. In this chapter we'll see even more striking echoes of wisdom from India in Lucas's saga. There are rich parallels between Yoda's training of Luke to become a Jedi, a spiritual warrior for the galaxy, and Krishna's training of the military general Arjuna to become a spiritual warrior for India, as recorded in the *Bhagavad Gita*.

Arjuna was the greatest archer of his time, a highly evolved and righteous military leader who was mentally paralyzed by the dilemma that he faced. His people were being attacked by evil-doers who also happened to *be* his people—namely, his cousins and uncles. If he did nothing to defend his civilization, it would be overrun by his family, which was bent on destroying his culture. If he defended his country, as he was trained to do and swore to do, he would be forced to kill his own flesh and blood. No wonder he was completely at a loss as to what to do when the story of the *Bhagavad Gita* opens. In confusion and supplication, he fell to his feet and asked Krishna to teach him what he should do to resolve what appeared to him as an insurmountable dilemma.

> *"My nature smitten with the taint of weakness, confused in mind about dharma, I pray Thee, tell me decisively what is good for me. I am Thy disciple; teach me for I have taken refuge in Thee."*
> —Chapter 2, verse 7

Before he did that, Krishna, the incarnation of God as preserver of the Universe, told both warring armies that they could choose to have either Krishna's charioteers or Him on their side, but that he Himself wouldn't lift a finger to actually fight. As an expression of his highly developed moral and spiritual nature, Arjuna chose God, while his enemies happily opted for God's vast fighting army. From a 1981 *Revenge of the Jedi* story conference transcript, with series creator George Lucas, writer Lawrence Kasdan, director Richard Marquand, and producer Howard Kazanjian, Lucas said: "Yoda teaches Jedi, but he is like a guru; he doesn't go out and fight anybody." Krishna taught Arjuna to fight, as well, but he himself stayed out of the fray.

Krishna undertook the spiritual education of Arjuna, first by explaining the nature of life and death and the indestructible nature of the eternal soul.

> *"You grieve for those whom there should be no grief, yet speak as do the wise. Wise men grieve neither for the dead nor for the living. There never was a time when I was not, nor you, nor these rulers of men. Nor will there ever be a time when all of us shall cease to be. As the dweller in the body passes into childhood, youth and age, so also does he pass into another body. This does not bewilder the wise."*
> —Chapter 2, verses, 11-13

He expanded on this teaching four verses later, when he said,

"None can work the destruction of this immutable Being."

Later on, he would put forth the teaching of dharma (Sanskrit for the cosmic Force which upholds evolution and righteousness). As a military protector, it was Arjuna's dharma (social role) to protect society against such evil, no matter who the perpetrator of that negativity happened to be. So in the next verse, Krishna would add the following teaching:

> *"These bodies are known to have an end; the dweller in the body is eternal, imperishable, infinite, Therefore, O Bharata, fight!"*
> —Chapter 2, verse 18

Krishna expanded on his theme by telling Arjuna in unequivocal terms:

> *"Do your allotted duty. Action indeed is superior to inaction."*
> —Chapter 3, verse 8

Before the second chapter comes to a close, Krishna teaches Arjuna meditation, and gives the general the spiritual experience of the timeless, eternal nature of his very own soul.

> *"The Vedas' concern is with the three gunas. Be without the three gunas, O Arjuna, freed from duality, ever firm in purity, independent of possessions, possessed of the Self."*
> —Chapter 2, verse 45

In *The Ramayana*, Vishvamitra Muni, as Rama's spiritual master, taught the great avatar (incarnation of God) in the forest to be adept in the art of war, but he also taught him that fighting must always be based on yogic principles. In *The Mahabharata*, Dronacharya trained the righteous Pandavas, of whom Arjuna was one, to be righteous yogi protectors of the innocent. Yoda is very much in the tradition of these two great Yoga masters.

Anger, Krishna says, leads to bewilderment, and bewilderment to loss of memory. At this point, the avatar explained, intelligence is lost. Yoda would sound a similar message to his disciple Luke Skywalker: "Fear leads to anger, anger leads to hate, hate leads to suffering." Fear, the diminutive Jedi master added, is also the path to the dark side.

YOGI YODA

The audience is unable to see the inner experiences of Luke Skywalker as Yoda's spiritual training of the aspirant evolved. We do eventually hear, as did he, that he, too, must kill his own flesh and blood, the father who created him. Anakin Skywalker, in whom the Force was highly developed before he was seduced by its dark side, had become Darth Vader, more of a machine than a man, and who was the merciless killing lieutenant for the evil Emperor. Obi-Wan Kenobi had taught Luke that the Jedis "were the guardians of peace and justice in the Old Republic," so, as a Jedi in training, it became Luke's dharma to restore harmony and peace to the galaxy. To do that, he had to overcome Darth Vader; he had to kill his very own father, much like Arjuna had to kill his own cousins and uncles. As Obi-Wan made abundantly clear: "There is no avoiding the battle. You must face and destroy Vader!"

But such killing wasn't to take place until the Jedi training was complete. Arjuna, who was to learn Yoga from Krishna and experience his own eternal nature on the battlefield, had his deep spiritual inner revelations before he had to go into the battle to fight. As audience members, we see the importance of meditation prior to doing battle in *The Phantom Menace*. Qui-Gon was chasing the evil Darth Maul, with deadly rays flying around. The Jedi chose to wait before he could move down the next corridor to vanquish his adversary. While his apprentice, the young Obi-Wan paced nervously, he sat and actually meditated. In other words, even in the very heat of battle, the Jedi fighter accepted the moment as it was, and meditated on it, without fighting it.

During his training, Luke asked his Master how he would be able to distinguish the light side from the dark side of the Force. Yoda told him that when his mind is "calm, at peace" such clarity would be present. Yoda taught Luke to control his senses and overcome desire and anger, very much like Krishna did with Arjuna. "[The midi-chlorians] continually speak to us, telling us the will of the Force," says Qui-Gon Jinn in *The Phantom Menace*. "When you learn to quiet your mind, you'll hear them speaking to you."

Krishna addressed that similar inner state when he told Arjuna that:

> *"The sage, whose senses, mind and intellect are controlled, whose aim is liberation, from whom desire, fear and anger have departed, is indeed forever free."*
>
> — Chapter 5, verse 28

Coming to live in the light side of the Force brings calmness and peace, Luke was told. We can't feel the peace and calmness that grew in the young Skywalker, but there was clearly enough of those qualities for him to advance in the awakening of the latent powers that will be discussed in chapter 14. We do glimpse a piece of Yoda's Jedi training of Luke as we see below.

> *"Concentrate… feel the Force…flow. Yes. Good. Calm, yes. Through the Force, things you will see. Other places. The future…the past."*

There are several types of Yoga that are elucidated by Krishna as part of his teaching of Arjuna. These include Jnana Yoga, Karma Yoga, and Bhakti Yoga. Translated, they are respectively the Yoga of Wisdom, cultivating the finest values of the mind; the Yoga of devotion through the expansion of love in the heart; and the Yoga of action through the doing of service. I bring up these paths of Yoga here because it appears to me as if Yoda was teaching Luke different aspects of these paths without necessarily naming them so to either Luke or to us, the audience.

Jedis in training, we discover, spend years studying texts to grow in knowledge. They also aspire to cultivate unconditional love for all beings. And lastly, they serve their society by keeping the peace and, if necessary, going to war to defend their people.

"Holding on to anger is like grasping a hot coal with the intent of throwing it at someone else; you are the one who gets burned."

— The Buddha

CHAPTER 5
THE BUDDHA & YODA

Many people who've seen the *Star Wars* saga have seen parallels between George Lucas's concept of the Force and the Buddha's teaching of the Dharma. Bill Moyers, in his interview with Lucas for a *Time* Magazine story, said,

> *"You said you put the Force into* Star Wars *because you wanted us to think on these things. Some people have traced the notion of the Force to Eastern views of God—particularly Buddhist—as a vast reservoir of energy that is the ground of all of our being. Was that conscious?"*

The filmmaker's response was far more spiritual than it was cinematic.

> *"I guess it's more specific in Buddhism, but it is a notion that's been around before that. When I wrote the first* Star Wars, *I had to come up with a whole cosmology: What do people believe in? I had to do something that was relevant, something that imitated a belief system that has been around for thousands of years, and that most people on the planet, one way or another, have some kind of connection to. I didn't want to invent a religion. I wanted to try to explain in a different way the religions that have already existed. I wanted to express it all."*

"The quest for peace, for justice—I can apply Buddhism to those themes very easily," says Matthew Bortolin, author of *The Dharma of Star Wars*. The great spiritual teacher Yoda reminds many people of an iconoclastic Zen master.

"In the saga, a lot of the dialogue is about mindfulness, concentration, letting go and just the general meditation," says Bortolin, an educational consultant who waited some 30 hours to see the first midnight show of *Revenge of the Sith* in Los Angeles. "Meditation is confronting ourselves and the Dark Side elements within us," he says "Buddhism is about the human condition."

WHAT'S IN A NAME?

Even some of the names that Lucas used for his characters and regions of his universe are remarkably similar to Buddhist terms. The love of the pivotal character in the story—Anakin Skywalker—who becomes the mother of Luke and Leia, is named Padme Amidala. Her first name is eerily similar to the word padma, which means lotus in Sanskrit. In the Hindu tradition, out of which the Buddha was raised, a lotus flower came out of the navel of the god Vishnu holding the god Brahma. (Vishnu is God in His form of maintainer of creation, while Brahma is God as creator.) Perhaps the most well known mantra in Buddhist circles is "Om mani padme hum." These similarities in names seem far too close to be purely accidental. But that's not all. Amidala, her last name, is quite similar to the word Amida, a name of the celestial Buddha in Japan's Pure Land sect of Buddhism, also known as Amitabha.

Luke is initiated into the Jedi mysteries on the planet Dagobah; dagoba is a Buddhist meditation sitting area. The name Jedi is also very close to that of Jodo—Jodo Shinshu is a school in the sect of Pure Land Buddhism. Again, these similarities are far too close to be considered just coincidences, especially since Lucas referred to himself as a "Buddhist Methodist." The *Star Wars* creator also hired Irvin Kershner, a student of Zen Buddhism, to direct *The Empire Strikes Back*, the film in which the Buddha-like Yoda played such a pivotal role in the spiritual training of Luke, and the development of the series' plot.

While I'm not suggesting that Yoda was as evolved a teacher as the Buddha—although he did live 900 years and had extraordinary mental abilities—it is clear that Yoda was teaching Luke Skywalker — and many young Jedis in training before him—a spiritual path akin to that of the Buddha's. The Jedi gnome with the Yoga-like name taught a combination of concentration and mindfulness to his young Jedi charges, a combination that's quite similar to practices prescribed by the Buddha that are still being practiced today. Compassion is a key element in the Buddhist tradition; it's what kept the Buddha teaching aspirants instead of going off to enjoy Nirvana by himself in the forest without the busyness of social intercourse and the virtually endless activity of teaching. It's also the driving force behind the Bodhisattva vow, which is to continue teaching the Dharma and delay their own enlightenment until all beings can attain Nirvana. That's a level of compassion and commitment to others that's virtually unlimited and unknown elsewhere in our world.

Luke Skywalker demonstrated quite a lot of compassion, as well, when he gave up fighting Darth Vader, the embodiment of pure evil. He did this because he believed that there was still goodness in the man who succumbed to the dark side of the Force. Luke allowed himself to be imprisoned by Vader's master, the evil Emperor, so as to get close to this man who fathered him. This belief in Vader's goodness was a radical departure from Luke's own teachers—Yoda and Obi-Wan Kenobi, two great Jedi masters—who were convinced that Vader was unredeemable, and therefore had to be killed by Luke with no ifs, ands, or buts. The dialogue between Luke and Anakin ran as follows:

Luke: "You were once Anakin Skywalker, my father."
Vader: "That name no longer has any meaning for me."
Luke: "It is the name of your true self. You've only forgotten. I know there is good in you."

Luke said this to a Jedi knight who had slaughtered innocent young Jedis in training to prove his allegiance to his new Sith master years earlier. And so Luke continued to implore Vader: "Search your feeling, Father. Let go of your hate."

And as Vader turned his attention within at the request of his only son, he found himself once again—Anakin Skywalker—who was devoted to become a great Jedi knight. So Luke was right: not only did Vader demonstrate goodness at the end of his life; he then went one giant step further and killed the evil Emperor as his last act before dying. As Vader lay on the floor breathing his last, Luke wanted to somehow save this once great man. Vader 's response was apt and wise: You have already saved me." Luke was speaking literally; his father figuratively. The dying words are reminiscent of Christ's words on the cross to the criminal who was dying on a cross next to him: "Truly, I say to you, today you shall be with Me in Paradise." (Luke 23:43)

FREEDOM FROM ATTACHMENT

Buddha taught that attachment to impermanence was the principal cause of suffering; or what he referred to as dukkha. Anakin pointed out to his beloved Padme that attachment is taboo among the Jedis, as well. He said to this woman, for whom the fires of passion burned in him, "Attachment is forbidden. Possession is forbidden." His strong psychic vision which showed him that his beloved would eventually die in childbirth—she did—coupled with his fear of that spurred him to succumb to the promise of the evil Sith Emperor Palpatine, who claimed that he could teach Anakin the dark side of the Force and conquer the death that he foresaw for his bride.

COMMITMENT

It took tremendous commitment to stay one-pointed on the Jedi path of training; masters showed little patience for their disciples' waffling. When Yoda told Luke to raise a rocket ship with his mind alone, Luke said he would try, despite the outrageousness of his teacher's request. That's when the ancient one replied with his famous maxim: "Do or do not. There is no try." The demand and the quote are both reminiscent of some of the outrageous teaching methods practiced by dozens of masters in the Zen tradition throughout the ages. The force of will required to comply with Yoda's wishes is also reminiscent of the kind of overwhelming force of will demonstrated by Gautama, who sat under the bodhi tree and resolved not to get up until he became enlightened. It is that sheer determination—along with his resistance to the many temptations presented to him by demons such as Mara—that transformed Gautama into the Buddha, the Awakened One. Far fewer temptations than that brought Anakin to the dark side of the Force (see chapter 9), and similar ones—also resisted—turned Jesus into the Christ (chapter 8).

Concentration plays a critical role in the Buddhist meditation methods, and it does in a Jedi's training regimen, as well. "Don't center on your anxieties…keep your concentration here and now where it belongs," Qui-Gon Jinn said to Obi-Wan in his early spiritual development. Years later, when Yoda was teaching Luke, he uttered a similar dictum to his young charge: "Concentrate…Feel the Force flow." It was this lack of concentration that Yoda saw in the young Skywalker that prevented him from wanting to teach Luke at that time, despite Obi-Wan's strong request to the contrary. "Never his mind on where he was. What he was doing," Yoda told Obi-Wan about the youth, implying that it was where he would be going that was of greater importance to the youth.

LETTING GO

As central a role in the practice of Buddhist mindfulness meditation that concentration occupies, so too, does the latter idea of letting go. Since attachment is the principle cause of suffering, letting go of such clinging begins the process of awakening. Learning how to allow things to simply be instead of always willing them to happen opens one to Reality or the Force. Obi-Wan reminded Luke of this as the latter was poised to shoot the evil Empire's Death Star out of existence. But his desire to destroy was so strong, his quest to be a hero so powerful, that a disembodied Obi-Wan had to come out of the other world—he had already died—to tell his young charge to "Use the Force, Luke, let go." The young Skywalker did just that, and let the Force destroy the Death Star with an accurate shot that he probably would not have succeeded at doing if he used his will alone.

WE'RE ALL ONE

The interconnectedness that is such a strong principle in Buddhism is also expressed in the Jedi training. As Yoda was quoted as saying earlier in this book (See chapter 1.):

> *"You must feel the Force around you. Here, between you...me...the tree... the rock...everywhere? Yes, even between the land and the ship!"*

It's this oneness among all life forms, this interconnectedness, that inspired Luke to risk his life to save the lives of others.

*"When the highest type of men hear Tao,
they diligently practice it.
When the average type of men hear Tao,
they half believe in it.
When the lowest type of men hear Tao,
they laugh heartily at it."*

— Lao Tzu

"But everyone who hears these words of mine and does not put them into practice is like a foolish man who built his house on sand."

— Matthew 7:26

CHAPTER 6
THE FORCE & THE TAO

When we first met Han Solo, he was like the man who Lao Tzu described who either laughs at the Tao or only half believes in it. Consider, after all, what he said to his across-the-galaxy flying clients Luke Skywalker and Obi-Wan Kenobi about the Force, which they both very much believed in:

> *"Hokey religions and ancient weapons are no match for a good light blaster at your side, kid...I've flown from one side of this galaxy to the other. I've seen a lot of strange stuff, but I've never seen anything to make me believe there's one all-powerful Force controlling everything. No mystical energy field controls my destiny. It's all a lot of simple tricks and nonsense."*

As the *Star Wars* saga unfolds, Han evolved as well, and didn't go solo in his romantic life, creating a child with Princess Leia.

The Force in George Lucas's *Star Wars* films and the Tao of Taoism have a number of things in common. "One way to describe the Force is the universal energy that surrounds all beings and connects everything—that's the Tao," says John Porter, author of *The Tao of Star Wars*.

The Tao is said to contain the opposite forces of light and dark energies in the universe as pictorially illustrated in the famous yin/yang circle of light in the dark half circle and dark in the half circle of light. The Force, of course, is characterized as having a light side and a dark. The heroes of Lucas's space fairy tale serve the light side of the force; the evil ones serve their own egos with the aid of the dark side. Anakin Skywalker was a hero when he served the light side, but became a deadly monster after he was seduced by the dark side and succumbed to its temptations. He then gave his allegiance to It and to the evil Emperor, who he then served.

In the Chinese Taoist tradition, those with superhuman abilities are called Junzi. Yoda was clearly such a being, as was Luke after he learned from the ancient Jedi master many of the secrets of the light side. Obi-Wan Kenobi was a talented Junzi in the *Star Wars* prequel, evolved still further to become a noble Daojun, as a Taoist might put it, when he took on Anakin as his first disciple. He rose even further into the status of a Shengren, or what the Chinese would call a sage. At last, he grew into the status of immortality (Xianren)—a status also enjoyed by the 900-year-old Yoda—when he let himself die to save Luke and his fellow rebels against the Empire. Obi-Wan also became a guiding spirit (Shen) for Luke, often manifesting in his spirit form, to continue to teach his former disciple. All the Jedis were trained in combat that looked awfully similar to the Chinese martial arts that have been practiced by many Taoists.

THE WAY OF WU-WEI

One of the most important precepts in the Taoist classic, *The Tao Te Ching*, by Lao Tzu, is the notion of wu-wei. This is often translated as non-action in the spirit of effortless behavior. It is not passivity or lethargy at all. It is effortless activity that springs from the center of one's being, one's essential nature or Te.

During Luke's Jedi training program with the ancient Yoda the youth often used his will instead of letting things be, and letting the Force do the work. At one point, when the master asked the disciple to raise a rocket ship, the overwhelmed youth said that he'd try. That's when the teacher shot back his now-famous dictum: "There's do or not do, there's no try." The Tao doesn't try, the sun doesn't try, and neither does a tiger in the jungle, poised to make an attack and a kill. Each is centered in its nature, and allows Nature to express Itself through it. That is also what the disembodied Obi-Wan encouraged his charge to do when he was using technology instead of the Force to destroy the Empire's Death Star as we saw in the previous chapter: "Use the Force, Luke, let go." Letting go enabled the youth to become one with the Force and take a shot from there. He did, and the shot was successful, destroying this deadly weapon in the hands of the evil Emperor.

While Luke Skywalker, prior to undertaking his Jedi training with Yoda, would not have resonated with the wisdom teachings of Lao Tzu, in time, through the esoteric training from his very Taoist-like spiritual master, he would come to understand and even embody some of the great truths brought to the world through this ancient Chinese wisdom tradition.

"The Lord your God will raise up a Prophet like me from among your own people. Listen carefully to everything He tells you. Anyone who will not listen to that Prophet will be cut off from God's people and utterly destroyed."

— Moses

CHAPTER 7
SKYWALKERS & DESERT WALKERS: JUDAISM & JEDIISM

Star Wars tells the story of a galaxy far, far away, but in this galactic tale there are also many echoes of a Middle Eastern people long, long ago. While I don't suggest that there's a conscious borrowing from the history of Judaism by George Lucas—he himself is not descended from one of the 12 tribes—there are some strong parallels between the ancient Jews and the extra terrestrial Jedis. The similarities probably have more to do with archetypal influences from the Collective Unconscious than from any direct borrowing by the filmmaker from the *Torah* or the *Talmud*.

How did small groups of rebels like the Israelites and the heroes in the *Star Wars* saga prevail against such larger foes? It's not through the support of a big army that would have any enemy quake in its boots, but by an invisible Force known in cinematic terms, as the Force, and in the *Old Testament* as God.

Those who know something of Jewish history know of the Hanukkah tale of an event some 2,200 years ago, when the Israelites miraculously overcame the tyranny of the Seleucid Empire. Going further back into Jewish history we read of the story of the Exodus, in which a group of powerless slaves gained liberation from a powerful evil empire of Egyptians through the intervention of a Cosmic Force called God who worked miracle after miracle through his emissary Moses.

The *Old Testament* also records the miraculous story of a young Israelite named David—youngest of Jesse's eight sons—armed with nothing but a slingshot and five smooth stones, who risked his life to battle the Philistine giant Goliath, who stood 9 feet, 9 inches, and wore a bronze suit of armor that weighed 125 pounds. Whoever won the fight would have his people rule over the loser's people.

Saul, the leader of the Israelites, said to David, son of his servant, "Go, and the Lord be with you." God similarly encouraged Joshua, who led the Hebrew people to the Promised Land after the death of Moses, when he said, "Be strong and courageous; do not be frightened or dismayed, for the Lord your God is with you wherever you go." (Joshua 1:9) This pair of passages from the Bible clearly presage the *Star Wars* expression, "May the Force be with you."

Back to our story. Upon meeting each other to do battle, David said to the giant, "You come against me with sword and spear and javelin, but I come against you in the name of the LORD Almighty, the God of the armies of Israel, whom you have defied." (1 Samuel 17:45)

The defeat of Goliath by David has become the inspiration for the expression of David and Goliath contests in which a small underdog somehow manages to vanquish a giant powerhouse. We use this metaphor in sports, in politics, and business. The rebels in *Star Wars* are like outer space Davids defeating the Empire's Death Star with little more than a little bit of weaponry and an awful lot of moxie.

HEBREWS IN OUTER SPACE?

The name Yoda sounds somewhat like "yada," (not to be confused, with yada, yada, yada, my fellow *Seinfeld* fans) which is translated in Hebrew as "to know." The name Leia sounds awfully like Leah, wife of the Hebrew patriarch Jacob. Linguists have looked at the breastplate of Darth Vader and seen it as Hebrew lettering upside down as "One shall be regarded innocent until he is proven guilty," according to Seth Rogovoy, writing for *The Forward* online in "The Secret Jewish History of Star Wars," at http://forward.com/culture/327265/the-secret-jewish-history-of-star-wars/.

Moses' 40-year journey through the desert, an exodus out of Egypt to the Promised Land, took place through the arid desert. As the Israelites wandered through this deserted area, they confronted one obstacle after another but were always saved by Cosmic Intelligence, the Force they believed in and worshipped and referred to as God.

THE PROPHETS & THE JEDIS

In the long Jewish tradition, prophets, who acted as mouthpieces for God, were forever arising to bring a more cosmic point of view among the people, who often lost their spiritual sensibilities. The great seer Isaiah, for example, foresaw the coming of a Messiah who would have his way prepared (Isaiah 40:3-5); would be born of a virgin (Isaiah 7:4); would have a Galilean ministry (Isaiah 9:1-2), and so forth.

Among Jedis in the *Star Wars* saga, there was a prophecy of one who would bring balance to the Force. Mace Windu said to Qui-Gon Jinn of the latter's young protégé, Anakin Skywalker:

"If the prophecy is true, your apprentice is the only one who can bring the Force back into balance."

Like the Hebrew prophets who had inner vision and could see the future, the youthful Anakin "can see things before they happen," his mentor told the Jedi council of knights.

Whereas Moses found God in a burning bush, Yoda taught Luke to feel the Force among the trees and in all of Nature.

In the *Bible*, we read, "Trust in the Lord with all your heart, and do not rely on your own insight. In all your ways acknowledge him, and he will make straight your paths." (Proverbs 3:5-6) Luke was taught by a disembodied Obi-Wan to "Use the Force Luke, let go, Luke."

The *Old Testament* has long reminded the Hebrew people that "Ye shall be as gods." (Genesis 3:5) and "Be still and know that I am God." (Psalm 46:10) Yoda made certain that Luke would be able to know the light side of the Force from its dark side when you are "calm, at peace." And he proceeded to show him how to gain that inner peace, of which the Hebrew scriptures sang so beautifully.

> "*Remember, the Force will be with you always.*"
> — Obi-Wan Kenobi

> "*And remember, I am with you always, to the end of the age.*"
> — Jesus, (Matthew 28:20)

CHAPTER 8
THE GOSPEL OF LUKE (SKYWALKER): JESUS & THE JEDIS

In Jedi mythology, the highest good is achieved by balancing light and dark, whereas Christians believe the highest good is achieved when darkness is defeated. In Christianity, the dark side is not just the opposite of light, but is an unequal opponent of God, who, in *Star Wars* terms, is the Lord over the Force.

"The image of an out-of-the-way place, the birth of a child, the promised one, the one that provides hope—there are a lot of parallels to the birth of Christ," says Dick Staub, author of *Christian Wisdom of the Jedi Masters*.

I'm not the only person to devote a Sunday church sermon to *Star Wars*. The legendary Zion Church in Berlin, where theologian Dietrich Bonhoeffer worked in the 1930s, dedicated one of its Sundays to the sci-fi franchise as episode 7 of the *Star Wars* saga was about to hit German movie screens.

While there's much, of course, that is different about Jesus Christ and Luke Skywalker, they do share some things in common. A wise man, riding on top of an animal that looks something like a camel, rides in from the desert. That's an image common to both. An infant male child is brought to a couple who would become his adoptive parents. The boy was perhaps the "chosen one" of prophecy who would bring peace and harmony to the world. Are the elements of this scene a coincidental accident or was George Lucas consciously using Luke Skywalker as a symbol for Jesus Christ?

Both Luke and Jesus were raised by men who were not their real fathers. Both worked to restore harmony and justice in their worlds. Both underwent spiritual training to undertake their work. Both had a deep connection to a spiritual force that inspired their undertakings.

In the *Star Wars* space opera, Darth Vader (Anakin Skywalker) killed the evil Emperor and gave up his life in the process to save his son Luke, while in the *New Testament*, Jesus gave up his own life, so that his Father might live in all people as a Holy Spirit. Anakin was like a fallen Adam redeemed by Luke as a kind of forgiving Christ figure who saw light in Vader's black heart when even great Jedi masters such as Yoda and Obi-Wan saw him as unredeemable. Vader's sacrifice redeemed him and helped to restore harmony in the universe, while in the Gospels, Jesus' sacrifice redeemed all of humanity. As his father lay dying in his arms, Luke was asked by him to remove the Darth Vader mask so that he may look upon his boy with "my own eyes." The request was very reminiscent of a line from the *New Testament*, when Paul said,

> *"For now we see only a reflection as in a mirror; then we shall see face to face."*
>
> —1 Corinthians 13:12

After Vader's death, there was a funeral pyre and his body was cremated. The scene is shot at night with fires lighting up the evening sky. It, too, is reminiscent of a line from the Gospel of John, which said,

> *"The light shines in the darkness, and the darkness has not overcome it."*
>
> —John 1:5

A MESSIAH

Jedi prophecy had long held that one would come one day to bring cosmic order. When told of the great psychic gifts of young Anakin Skywalker, the Jedi knight Mace Windy said to Qui-Gon Jinn, the boy's discoverer and mentor:

> *"You're referring to the prophecy of the one who will bring balance to the Force...You believe it's this boy? Bring him before us, then...If the prophecy is true, your apprentice is the only one who can bring the Force back into balance."*

Throughout the *Old Testament*'s Book of Isaiah (see the preceding chapter) the prophet continually foresaw the coming of the Messiah to bring peace and freedom to the Hebrew people. As Jesus himself said, "For the Son of Man came to seek out and to save the lost." (Luke 19:10) It is prophesied in Isaiah that the Messiah would be born of a virgin; Anakin's mother claimed that he was conceived without a father. The parallels between Jesus and young Anakin continue: the former was said to have more of the Holy Spirit in him than any other man (John 3:34), while Anakin had a higher midi-chlorian count than anyone ever, anywhere in the galaxy.

Jesus' mission was to help people connect to the Kingdom of God within them and outside of them. Jedis were trained to connect to the Force that could be felt within and penetrated the outer world, as well. Obi-Wan taught that the Force "surrounds us, it penetrates us, it binds the galaxy together." The apostle Paul spoke of "one God and Father of all, who is over all and through all and in all." (Ephesians 4:6) "He is before all things, and in him all things hold together." (Collosians, 1:17)

Deep peace comes to those who connect with the Force and with God. Yoda told Luke that he would know the light side of the Force from the dark when you are "calm, at peace." Anakin said "to control your anger is to be a Jedi." Jesus taught people the "peace that passes all understanding." But to get to that peace, the mind has to be transformed. As Jesus put it, "Be not conformed to this world, but be transformed by the renewing of your mind." (Romans 12:2) Anakin, while he was still devoted to the light side of the Force, said, "Sometimes when you believe something to be real, it becomes real." Chapters 18 and 19 of this book teach a powerful method to transform your mind.

Great things can occur when one's belief in the Force and in God is strong. Yoda told Luke that he could move a rocket ship with his mind. Jesus told his followers that they could move mountains. Obi-Wan said that, "The Force also obeys your command." Jesus demonstrated that the high winds on a stormy sea could actually calm down, obeying his command, as well. When he commanded water to turn into wine, or inspired crippled legs to walk, and blind eyes to see, and demons to leave the bodies of suffering humanity, they did just that.

Both Jesus and Yoda spoke about the power of belief, as well as the danger that comes with doubt. "That is why you fail," Yoda told Luke when the latter said he couldn't believe that a rocket could be lifted by consciousness alone. When Peter, the apostle, was walking on water, and then suddenly couldn't believe that he could perform such a miracle even though he already was, he began to sink. "You of little faith," Jesus said, "why did you doubt?" (Matthew 14:31)

Entering Heaven, Jesus taught, was through a combination of transforming one's belief system, purifying one's heart to its original innocence, and having faith in God. Jesus put it this way:

> *"Truly, I say to you, whoever does not receive the Kingdom of God like a child shall not enter it."*
>
> —Luke, 18:17

Yoda spoke of this childlike innocence, as well. "You must unlearn what you learned," he told Luke, if he was to become successful in his training. He added: "Truly wonderful the mind of a child is."

Attachment is also an ingredient. Jesus said, "None of you can become my disciple if you do not give up your possessions." (Luke 14:33) Anakin told his beloved Padme, "Attachment is forbidden. Possession is forbidden."

People are quick to believe that George Lucas modeled the Force and much of the spirituality in his *Star Wars* space opera after the wisdom teachings of the East, as we've seen in chapters 4, 5, and 6. Fewer still, however, see much of a connection between the saga's spirituality and that of the teachings of Christ. Perhaps this chapter will change those beliefs. When Lucas admitted that he was a Methodist Buddhist, the Buddhist part was clear to many. Perhaps the Methodist part will be now, as well.

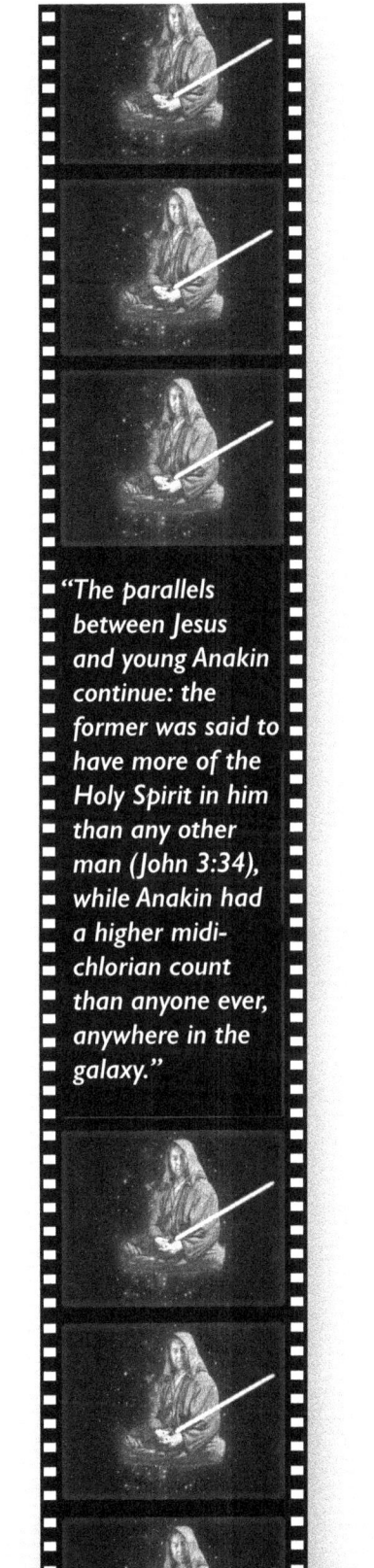

"The parallels between Jesus and young Anakin continue: the former was said to have more of the Holy Spirit in him than any other man (John 3:34), while Anakin had a higher midi-chlorian count than anyone ever, anywhere in the galaxy."

"When thine eye is single, thy whole body also is full of light; but when thine eye is evil, thy body also is full of darkness."

— Luke 11:34

CHAPTER 9
SATAN & THE DARK SIDE OF THE FORCE

The Judeo-Christian story about Lucifer (later renamed Satan, meaning adversary) is that he was once an angel who, because of his desire to compete with God, fell from Heaven. In more colloquial terms, he was much more into his own ego than in serving the Almighty, as the other angels were.

> *"For you [Lucifer] have said in your heart, I will ascend into heaven, I will exalt my throne above the stars of God: I will sit also upon the mount of the congregation, in the sides of the north."*
> —Isaiah 14:13

And so he was kicked out of Heaven after the failure of his "coup d' God," and banished to the earth of which he has dominion. In the *Bible*, he is referred to as the "god of this world." (II Corinthians 4:4) "I beheld Satan as lightning fall from heaven," Christ said. (Luke 10:18) The evil one is content to rule over Hell and draw as many souls from the Earth into his underworld home. Had Anakin Skywalker been a character in the *Bible* he clearly would have been swayed into Satan's camp. Consider what he uttered even after his training had begun:

> *"I will be the most powerful Jedi ever! I promise you, I will even learn how to stop people from dying."*

Putting ego before the Force, glory before service, Anakin was clearly on the fast track to the dark side. The Sith, deeply versed in the dark arts, developed evil powers through surrender and allegiance to the dark side of the Force. If George Lucas had wanted to personify the Force's dark side, It could certainly have been Satan. But as the creator of the *Star Wars* saga put it, "All I was trying to say in a very simple and straightforward way is that there is a good and bad side."

It was Anakin's visions of the death of his beloved in childbirth that made him vulnerable to be seduced by the evil Sith. It was the young Jedi's fears that made him so susceptible. Fear, he was taught in his training program, leads one to the dark side. His son was also tempted by the evil Emperor Palpatine to leave the light side of the Force for the dark, but resisted, even though it would have meant his own death. As he told the Emperor, "I'll never turn to the dark side. You've failed, Your Highness." The temptation of Luke is a clear echo of the temptation of Jesus in the wilderness by Satan. In his interview with Lucas in *Time*, Bill Moyers asked:

> *"When Darth Vader tempts Luke to come over to the Empire side, offering him all that the Empire has to offer, I am taken back to the story of Satan taking Christ to the mountain and offering him the kingdoms of the world, if only he will turn away from his mission. Was that conscious in your mind?"*

The filmmaker replied:

> *"Yes. That story also has been retold. Buddha was tempted in the same way. It's all through mythology. The gods are constantly tempting everybody and everything. So the idea of temptation is one of the things we struggle against, and the temptation obviously is the temptation to go to the dark side. One of the themes throughout the films is that the Sith lords, when they started out thousands of years ago, embraced the dark side."*

When the Emperor Palpatine seduced Anakin Skywalker to the dark side of the Force, he not only promised to show him how to save his beloved Padme from death, he also promised his young potential disciple the most extraordinary gift of immortal life for himself, as well. Satan didn't promise Jesus immortal life, but he did attempt to tempt him with dominion over the whole world, a power that held absolutely no appeal to young Jesus. After resisting all three of the Devil's temptations, the latter left, and angels instead appeared in his place. As Jesus' apostle James put it, so succinctly, "Resist the devil and he will flee from you." (James 4:7) This was clearly not a piece of knowledge ever presented to Anakin Skywalker. Perhaps if he ever had the pleasure to learn of such a reality, he never would have become Darth Vader.

Chapter 9—Satan & the Dark Side of the Force

It's to George Lucas's credit that he had no need to introduce Satan or the Devil himself into his intergalactic saga. The evil Emperor and his lieutenant, Anakin Skywalker, who abandoned the light side of the Force and its ethical teachings for the dark side and its ego-enhancing lures, very much embodied such Satanic influences.

"Merlin, make me a hawk! Let me fly away from here."
— King Arthur, *Camelot*

CHAPTER 10
JEDI KNIGHTS & THE ROUND TABLE: *STAR WARS*, CAMELOT, & THE MIDDLE AGES

Because the *Star Wars* saga is an archetypal myth it's not surprising that there are similarities between it and that great Western myth that we know as Camelot. Luke was like a kind of galactic Arthur Pendragon, intent on creating justice in his world. Both Arthur and Luke were raised by men who were not their father, and both would eventually come to learn who their true father was. Great men told these young males about their true parentage: Obi-Wan told the Jedi knight Luke about his, and Merlin did the same for the young King Arthur, who inspired a round table of knights to sit with him.

Yoda and Obi-Wan Kenobi were Luke's shaman/wizard teachers, in an analogous way that Merlin was for the young king of the Britons. The light saber that Obi-Wan gave Luke, which had belonged to his onetime noble father, Anakin Skywalker, is akin to the magical Excalibur sword that Merlin inspired Arthur to pull out of the stone, which would ascend him to the throne of England.

Arthur and Luke were both asked to kill family members: Luke had to destroy his evil father Darth Vader, while King Arthur was impelled to kill his illegitimate son Mordred. He also had to decide the fate of his wife, Queen Guinevere, who cuckolded him through an adulteress affair with his best friend and most powerful knight, Sir Lancelot. Angered Britons demanded that she be burned at the stake.

The love triangle that existed among Luke, Leia, and Han, before Luke finally came to learn that the princess was actually his twin sister, also mirrored that of Arthur, Guinevere, and Lancelot. Ironically,

Lancelot's tremendous strength in battle was attributed to his lifelong chastity, an austerity that he would cast aside in his passion for his queen. Chastity, you'll recall, is one of the necessary features in the Jedi training program. The loss of chastity was also one of the indirect causes of the fall from grace of Anakin Skywalker. His marriage to, and sexual relationship with, Princess Amidala had to be kept secret because Jedis were to remain celibate and single.

Both Camelot and the rebellion against the evil Empire feature knights. One sat around a round table at Camelot, the other sat in a round-ish council manned by a number of Jedi knights. Both sets of knights were empowered to defend against evil, rather than to wage war. Both were also schooled in a variety of virtues; chivalry was one of the most famous ones of Arthur's knights.

In her book *The Persistence of Medievalism*, Angela Jane Weisl wrote,

> "while George Lucas likes to claim that Star Wars *is a myth for modern times, it is striking that among the variety of mythic narratives he suggests, his strongest inspiration is clearly the medieval Arthurian romance.*"

Writing in a blog entitled "Star Wars and the Middle Ages" (http://www.medievalists.net/2014/03/star-wars-middle-ages/), Peter Konleczny talked of three different kinds of Middle Ages influences on Lucas's concept of Jedi knights. The first two were from the Asian continent, the third from Europe. They were as follows: Shaolin Monks from 5th century China; Japanese Samurai; and the Knights Templar of the 12th to 14th centuries.

The Chinese monks' concept of Qi is a very likely influence on George Lucas's notion of the Force as a kind of invisible glue of the Universe that can be utilized for healing as well as for warfare, and which has a dark (yin) and light side (yang) which can be used constructively or destructively. A master synthesizer, Lucas pulled from traditions throughout the world and throughout human history to fashion his galaxy far, far away.

The Medieval scholar/blogger also cited the Samurai helmet as a very probable influence for the costume of Darth Vader. The Samurai, he pointed out, were disciples of Zen Buddhism, which taught, among other things, the necessity to transcend the activity of the conscious mind, the cultivation of mushin or "no mind," which will remind *Star Wars* fans of Obi-Wan's injunction to Luke when he said, "Let go of your conscious self and act on instinct."

The Knights Templar were such a powerful influence on Lucas's early thinking that the early scripts that he had written for *Star Wars* actually referred to his Jedi knights as Jedi Templar. You can't get a clearer influence than that. This Medieval group of monks, that inspired the filmmaker, were of the military stripe, and like the Jedis of *Star Wars*, they were celibate and obedient, and were highly esteemed for their integrity, courage and wisdom.

"There are mythical underpinnings to the movie and archetypes that have been around for thousands and thousands of years, most of them before Christianity."

— George Lucas

CHAPTER 11
A NEW MYTHOS FROM A GALAXY FAR, FAR AWAY

Soon after *Star Wars* first came out in movie theaters in 1977, almost every single religion suggested that the enormously popular motion picture gave cinematic expression to the teachings of their faith. Jews and Christians saw its parallels to stories in the *Old* and *New Testaments* in the *Bible*; Muslims saw similarities to the *Koran*; Hindus were able to hear echoes from the *Bhagavad Gita*; Buddhists noticed notions from the *Dhammapada*, and Chinese could see the Tao in Lucas's Force, for example. We've covered many of these overtones in preceding chapters. This is true because Lucas consciously did borrow from some of these traditions, but because the film is mythic in the deepest sense of the word, it conveys truths that are *universally* held, transcending the often-times exclusive claims of particular religions.

In a 1999 story in *Time* magazine called "Of Myth and Men," the journalist Bill Moyers interviewed George Lucas, and asked him to directly discuss both the mythic and religious elements of his work. Lucas responded:

> "*I don't see* Star Wars *as profoundly religious. I see* Star Wars *as taking all the issues that religion represents and trying to distill them down into a more modern and easily accessible construct—that there is a greater mystery out there. I remember when I was 10 years old, I asked my mother, 'If there's only one God, why are there so many religions?' I've been pondering that question ever since, and the conclusion I've come to is that all the religions are true.*"

Moyers followed up with this comment:

> *"One explanation for the popularity of* Star Wars *when it appeared is that by the end of the 1970s, the hunger for spiritual experience was no longer being satisfied sufficiently by the traditional vessels of faith."*

To which Lucas replied:

> *"I put the Force into the movie in order to try to awaken a certain kind of spirituality in young people—more a belief in God than a belief in any particular religious system. I wanted to make it so that young people would begin to ask questions about the mystery. Not having enough interest in the mysteries of life to ask the question, 'Is there a God or is there not a God?'—that is for me the worst thing that can happen. I think you should have an opinion about that. Or you should be saying, 'I'm looking. I'm very curious about this, and I am going to continue to look until I can find an answer, and if I can't find an answer, then I'll die trying.' I think it's important to have a belief system and to have faith."*

The hero journey has existed in literature, scripture, fairy tales, legends, and the like for millennia. In the middle of the 20th century, Joseph Campbell, the esteemed mythology professor at Sarah Lawrence College, wrote a groundbreaking book called *The Hero with a Thousand Faces* that clearly described the various stages of those journeys. The book would have a profound effect on George Lucas. In it, Campbell broke out the mythic adventure into three main phases, each of which contained specific events. These are:

1. The Departure;
2. The Initiation;
3. The Return.

In Campbell's nomenclature, the Departure features five steps. These are as follows:

1. The call to adventure;
2. Refusal of the call;
3. Aid from supernatural powers;
4. The crossing of the first threshold;
5. And finally the belly of the whale.

Chapter 11—A New Mythos from a Galaxy Far, Far Away

In a very lucid Internet article on *Star Wars* and Campbell (http://www.moongadget.com/origins/myth.html), Kristen Brennan interprets events in Lucas's saga into Campbell's structure. Luke's call to adventure came in a holographic message from Princess Leia that he received encoded in R2-D2's memory files. But as a farmer he had responsibilities to harvest his crop, so he chose not to do anything about rescuing some princess who he didn't even know. Obi-Wan Kenobi, who was blessed with supernatural powers, however, freed the young Skywalker from the sand people on Tattoine and told him how critical it was for the entire Empire that this royal rescue take place. The crossing of the threshold for Luke was his escape from the planet Tatooine after troops of the Empire burned down the home he had lived in, killing his uncle and aunt who had raised him after Obi-Wan had given the infant Luke to them immediately after his birth; his belly of the whale experience was his confinement in the garbage compactor on the Death Star.

Initiation began with trials, which for young Luke Skywalker was his beginning of light saber training. The hero journey usually then leads on to a meeting with a goddess or a god; for Luke, it was his encounter with Princess Leia, who earlier had been in an order of mystical training. The hero then is tempted; for Luke that meant the possible appeal of the dark side of the Force that so attracted his father a generation before. Atonement with the father often takes place next; in time, Luke and Darth Vader would enjoy an extraordinary peaceful rapprochement, despite their battle. Some heroes attain a status that partakes of the divine; for Luke that meant becoming a trained Jedi master with a number of supernatural abilities. Before returning home, the hero accomplishes a great boon for the world; in *Star Wars* Luke helped destroy the lethal Death Star of the Empire that threatened to destroy much of the galaxy, including the noble rebels who Luke fought with.

Some heroes refuse to return to their ordinary world, and Luke was no different, wanting to remain to avenge the murder of Obi-Wan. If the hero does return, his voyage is sometimes supported by the gods, and for Luke that meant transportation in the extraordinary freighter, the Millennium Falcon, which could fly in virtually miraculous ways including ".5 above light speed," according to its pilot, Han Solo. On their voyages home sometimes heroes need support by humans, as well, and Luke required the aid of Han, who rescued him from the evil clutches of Darth Vader. As the hero passes through the threshold of home, he may be confronted by even more of an opposition; the Millennium Falcon that transported Luke went on to kill The Imperial Empire fighter planes. Upon his safe return home, the hero is feted as a master of two worlds; in *Star Wars*, a victory ceremony was prepared to honor Luke. The hero's return means peace for his people, and in *Star Wars* that meant the rebellion that Luke played such a major role in was successful against the Evil Empire.

THE NEW MYTH

In an interview with George Lucas for *Time* Magazine, Bill Moyers said,

> *"Joseph Campbell once said all the great myths, the ancient great stories, have to be regenerated in every generation. He said that's what you are doing with* Star Wars. *You are taking these old stories and putting them into the most modern of idioms, the cinema. Are you conscious of doing that? Or are you just setting out to make a good action-movie adventure?"*

Lucas's response was telling:

> *"With* Star Wars *I consciously set about to re-create myths and the classic mythological motifs. I wanted to use those motifs to deal with issues that exist today. The more research I did, the more I realized that the issues are the same ones that existed 3,000 years ago. That we haven't come very far emotionally."*

In a Michelle Kinnucan blog, "What Star Wars Teaches Us," in Common Dreams.org (May 10, 2002, http://commondreams.org/cgi-bin/ print.cgi?file=/views02/0510-06.htm.) the filmmaker was quoted as saying,

> *"This is the kind of movie we need. There needs to be a kind of film that expresses the mythological realities of life—the deeper psychological movements of the way we conduct our lives."*

In that *Time* magazine interview, Lucas said, "We've always tried to construct some kind of context for the unknown." In doing his research, Lucas said, he sought embodiments of evil in Christian, Hindu, and

Chapter 11—A New Mythos from a Galaxy Far, Far Away

Greek traditions. When Moyers asked Lucas if he was consciously creating a new myth, he replied:

> *"I'm telling an old myth in a new way. Each society takes that myth and retells it in a different way, which relates to the particular environment they live in. The motif is the same. It's just that it gets localized. As it turns out, I'm localizing it for the planet. I guess I'm localizing it for the end of the millennium more than I am for any particular place."*

When Moyers said that critics had blasted Lucas for trivializing organized religions, devising a myth with no strings attached, the filmmaker countered:

> *"That's why I would hesitate to call the Force God. It's designed primarily to make young people think about the mystery. Not to say, 'Here's the answer.' It's to say, 'Think about this for a second. Is there a God? What does God look like? What does God sound like? What does God feel like? How do we relate to God?' Just getting young people to think at that level is what I've been trying to do in the films. What eventual manifestation that takes place in terms of how they describe their God, what form their faith takes, is not the point of the movie."*

The filmmaker was most definitely telling the timeless inner hero journey story that Campbell chronicled, only in outer space. As he told Moyers:

> *"Most myths center on a hero, and it's about how you conduct yourself as you go through the hero's journey, which in all classical myth takes the form of a voyage of transformation by trials and revelations. You must let go of your past and must embrace your future and figure out what path you're going to go down."*

"The Shadow knows."

— *The Shadow*, Walter Gibson, creator

CHAPTER 12
THE DARK SIDE & THE SHADOW: JUNG AT HEART

Jason Hamilton, who calls himself hooked on *Star Wars*, superheroes, and Shakespeare (a man, indeed, after my own heart), called Carl Jung "the great-grandfather of *Star Wars*."(http://www.starwars.com/news/star-wars-in-mythology-the-shadow) He dubbed the great Swiss Depth Psychologist this because his work in Analytical Psychology had a very deep impact on the great mythologist Joseph Campbell, who was unquestionably Lucas's biggest mentor. In fact, Lucas himself called Campbell "my Yoda." Hence, the indirect role that Jung played in the formation of Lucas's *Star Wars* cinematic universe.

Jung said that the Shadow is a part of the psyche that the conscious mind of a person refuses to recognize in himself, and so represses to the Unconscious. Its negative content doesn't sit well with the ego, so it gets locked up in the subconscious part of the mind, banished as it were. As Jung went on to say, "the less (the Shadow) is embodied in the individual's conscious life, the blacker and denser it is." Hamilton points to two famous literary examples in which the repressed Shadow temporarily takes over and wrecks havoc, violence, and death: namely Mr. Hyde in Robert Louis Stevenson's classic *The Strange Case of Dr. Jekyll and Mr. Hyde* and the legend of the werewolf.

The Force is depicted as having a light side and a dark side, and we see Luke Skywalker aspiring to live in the light, while his father, who once did just that, became seduced by the dark side because the Shadow overtook him. As blackness filled his being, he cut himself off from his gentle side and his humanity, and turned himself into an evil machine-like creature intent on violence and the destruction of all that we hold to be good and noble in life. The takeover by his Shadow was so complete that he literally took on a whole new name to depict the transformation: Darth Vader. A near-death light saber battle with Obi-Wan Kenobi—his former Jedi master and teacher—nearly obliterated his body and almost killed him. As a result, he became, through a complicated medical operation, something of a mechanical-like cyborg, having to breathe through a big black intricate mask.

Yoda taught Luke that to become a Jedi, a complete spiritual man, he must confront his Shadow side that was embodied in his own father. As the saying goes, "The apple doesn't fall far from the tree." So Luke recognized that, but for the grace of the Force, he might have gone the way of the dark side just like his father.

In a cave on the planet Dagobah, Luke had a kind of shamanic vision of Darth Vader; in it he had cut off the evil Sith's head. Moments later, he would realize that it was his own head that he had just cut off in the vision. This helped the young Jedi-in-training realize that Vader represented his own Shadow figure. The vision metaphor is apt: as Jung, Freud, and much of the field of psychology recognizes, the people in our dreams at night typically represent a part of ourselves.

While, in time, Luke came to love and accept his father (even the Shadow in Luke that Vader represented), he chose not to become like him, as he declared, "I'll never turn to the dark side...I am a Jedi." As Luke finally came to accept the Shadow within himself, Vader unpredictably abandoned his evil nature, and surprisingly killed the evil Emperor, his own master, who inspired him to renounce the light side for the dark in the first place. This act of treason spared his son's life. It was also an act of love, and would be his very last act, as well, dying in the presence of his son. He would die, though, heroically and at peace.

This was a radical choice by Darth Vader, who was sworn to destroy Jedis and to kill all those who were strong in the light side of the Force. But he wasn't only a rational being; he was also a father, and in that role he acted to save his son and kill his mentor. Those trained in the Force are taught to rely not only on reason and logic, but also on feelings. Clearly he was a father, who was acting on his feelings, just like the husband he was years ago who acted on his feelings to save his wife from dying in childbirth.

Luke Skywalker wasn't the only major character in the *Star Wars* saga who would have to confront his Shadow figure. While he made peace with it, his father did not until his final moments, demonstrating just how persistent and seductive the dark side, or the Shadow, can be. Anakin Skywalker was thought by members of the Jedi council to be the prophesied one who would bring balance to the Force. He had a midi-chlorian count in excess of 20,000, higher than any Jedi ever, including the 900-year-old Yoda. His mentor, Qui-Gon Jinn recognized that he could see things before they happened. He saw that, even as a young boy, Anakin Skywalker was unusually strong in the Force. So it was a huge shock to Obi-Wan Kenobi, who took over mentoring Anakin after Qui-Gon was killed in a light saber battle, when Anakin, as a young man, turned to the dark side and slaughtered Jedis, including young boys in training. There were hints, of course, all throughout Anakin's Jedi training that he would turn to the dark side. As moviegoers, we could see how he would turn out; this sad turn of events kept us munching even more actively on our bijou popcorn.

"Space...the final frontier."

— *Star Trek*

CHAPTER 13
STAR WARS & STAR TREK

When you consider that such a miniscule percentage of people who inhabit the Earth have ever left our terra firma for extra-planetary exploration, it's extraordinary that two of the most successful movie franchises in the history of the motion picture business have been *Star Wars* and *Star Trek*.

The latter, created by Gene Roddenberry, began as a television series in 1966 and ran for three seasons (79 episodes) on NBC-TV. Its five-year mission was "to explore strange new worlds, to seek out new life and new civilizations, to boldly go where no man has gone before." It was one of the most beloved TV programs ever, and has a loyal cadre of fans all these years later.

After the original series went off the air, it then morphed into four additional television programs: *Star Trek: The Next Generation* (1987-1994), *Star Trek: Deep Space Nine* (1993-1999), *Star Trek: Voyager* (1995-2001), and *Star Trek: Enterprise* (2001-2005). *Star Trek: Discovery* is set to debut on CBS All Access, a subscription streaming video on demand service, in 2017. There was also an animated series that ran for a year beginning in 1973.

There have also been 13 motion pictures, grossing more than $2.2 billion, from 1979 through 2016. A kind of mythic intergalactic *Gulliver's Travels*, the show sported influences from Greek, Roman, and Babylonian mythology. A number of the planets, people, and other living beings who Captain James Kirk and his crew, as well as the personnel on the other TV series, met up with were named after gods of Rome.

The original *Star Trek* series was nominated for 13 Emmy Awards; *Star Trek: The Next Generation* received one nomination; while *Star Trek: Deep Space Nine* hauled in four awards among its 32 nominations; and *Star Trek: Voyager* received seven Emmy Awards among its whopping 35 nominations. On the big screen, *Star Trek* films flew home with six of its 15 Oscar nominations.

Star Wars, which is set in a galaxy far, far away, also traces influences from the ancient mythologies of Greece and Rome, as well as Arthurian legend and the fictional Old English epic *Beowulf*, written about a thousand years after the birth of Christ. The tale tells of the heroic Beowulf, an earthly Luke Skywalker, who defeats the monstrous dragon Grendel, who was terrorizing his people.

The original film brought home six of the 10 Oscar nominations it was singled out for in the 1978 Oscar telecast; *The Empire Strikes Back* won two of its three nominations; *Return of the Jedi won* one of its four nominations; *The Phantom Menace* had three nominations; *Rogue One* had two, and *Attack of the Clones* and *Revenge of the Sith*, one apiece.

"Star Wars, which is set in a galaxy far, far away, also traces influences from the ancient mythologies of Greece and Rome, as well as Arthurian legend and the fictional Old English epic Beowulf."

"These superhero and mythical stories have, in many cases, replaced Biblical stories as vehicles for communal myths, but they are hardly any better than ancient magical adventures tinged with mythical archetypes and the decidedly un-nuanced black-and-white struggle between good and evil."

— Gudjon Bergmann,
More Likely to Quote Star Wars
than the Bible: Generation X and
Our Frustrating Search for
Rational Spirituality

CHAPTER 14
SUPERMAN, WOLVERINE, & YODA: JEDI KNIGHTS AS SUPERHEROES

There are even greater echoes of the wisdom of India contained in the *Star Wars* saga than were discussed in chapter 4. More than sixteen hundred years ago, a great yogi named Patanjali, in an effort to document the latent powers that are sleeping in all human beings, wrote *The Yoga Sutras*. His 196 aphorisms describe what these powers are, and how they can be awakened for use by aspirants. These abilities, found in abundance in comic book superheroes, include, but are not limited to, the main eight sidhis, or powers:

1. To become smaller than the smallest subatomic energy particles.
   We see this in the D.C. superhero Atom.
2. To become as expansive as the Universe itself.
   Marvel's Eternity can be anywhere and everywhere simultaneously.
3. To become like light.
   The Flash moves at virtually the speed of light.
4. To manifest any object.
   The Indian superhero Shaktimaan can manifest objects out of thin air. By the way, the word "shakti" in Sanskrit means power.
5. To fulfill any desire.
   Allenby Beardsley, also known as G Gundham, could manifest a variety of different superpowers simply through the desire to do just that.
6. To ostensibly transcend Nature's laws, such as walking on water or fire.
   Superman is probably the most famous embodiment of this sidhi with his ability to fly, while Aquaman, for example, can breathe under water.

7. To control others.
Comic book superheroes are usually so benign that they don't usually interfere with the free will of others, although the Shadow was able to cloud the minds of others. And Marvel's Karma could control the perceptions and actions of others, as well.
8. To be able to do anything.
The Marvel Comics character Infinity can know anything, for example.

The secret to manifesting these sidhis, or latent powers, the great Indian sage wrote, is *sanyama*, a Sanskrit term that translates loosely as subtle intentions from consciousness settled in *Samadhi*, the steady silent state of Being.

As the wisest of all Jedis, Yoda eventually showed Luke a number of these sidhis, including the ability to tap into the Force, or what different peoples on earth have called God, the Great Spirit, or the Tao, for example. In India, where Patanjali lived and taught, the name for that Great Spirit is Brahman. The sidhis that manifested for Luke in the *Star Wars* film saga were telepathy, levitation, clairvoyance, and psychokinesis, the latter being the ability to move physical objects with his mind alone. What's more, he could also influence the minds of others, and intuit the feelings of those nearby. In battle, he was able to sense what his opponent would do prior to him doing it, a huge advantage when battling for life and death. Also of great benefit to the benign warrior was the ability to engage in combat for many hours at a time without getting fatigued. Like the powerful X-Men hero Wolverine, Luke could also heal most any physical injury that he incurred, and quite quickly at that. This is an extraordinary skill for any fighter or warrior.

Luke's ability to levitate reminds us of the flying sidhi that we see manifested in such great comic book heroes as Superman, Captain Marvel, and many others who could conquer gravity.

Luke did confront a big obstacle during his training when Yoda, pleased that his pupil was growing in a number of sidhis, including psychokinesis, asked him to move a space ship with his mind alone. Such a sidhi comes easily to a number of X-Men, including Professor Xavier, Jean Gray, Magneto, and Psylocke. Other superheroes with this ability include Doctor Strange, Odin, Franklin Richards, and Matthew Malloy, among others.

Patanjali referred to the cultivation of certain spiritual virtues as facilitators of the sidhis. It appears that Jedi training includes these as well. They're known in Sanskrit as yamas and niyamas. Yamas are translated as a collection of "right living" or ethical guidelines; niyamas are thought of as right duties or observances.

The yamas that are vital to develop for the awakening of the sidhis in aspirants are:
- Satya (truthfulness);
- Asteya (non-stealing),;
- Brahmacharya (sexual energy control, celibacy);
- Aparigraha (non possessiveness or non-attachment);
- Ahimsa (non-violence).

The niyamas include:
- Shoucha (cleanliness or purity);
- Santosha (contentment);
- Tapas (austerity);
- Swadhyaya (self-study);
- Ishwara Pranidhana (surrender to God).

Attachment, or the art of letting go, is where the bright Jedi Anakin Skywalker faced his greatest challenge. He had visions of a future involving the death of his beloved wife in childbirth, shared that with his Master Yoda, who told him to let go of attachment, but Anakin refused to do so. And that is when he became susceptible to seduction by the dark side of the Force. Those who use the dark side feast on fear, aggression, and anger to gain their power, whereas the light side involves the use of knowledge, wisdom, understanding, meditation, asanas, acceptance, and ridding oneself of desire, etc.

Each and every one who aspires to become a Jedi knight is trained to follow such self-discipline as a way of purification if he is to become a proper Jedi. Yamas are practiced in a social setting, but these disciplines can be practiced anywhere including in isolation. At the end of episode 3 of the *Star Wars* saga, the sage Yoda went into isolation for a number of years, where he practiced all of these disciplines. There, he waited patiently for Luke to grow up, become ready to receive the training, and grow into the Jedi hero who would save the galaxy.

In most cases, caped superheroes like Superman and Captain Marvel, both in the comic books and on the silver screen, rarely pass on their superheroic talents to those in the next generation. (Exceptions include Batman, who trained Robin the Boy Wonder to assist him in his crime fighting, and the Amazon women on Paradise Island, who trained Wonder Woman, among others, to defend the planet against evil.) George Lucas is more in harmony with Yogi Patanjali in that the spiritual tradition that he created saw the wisdom in passing on this precious knowledge from one generation of Jedis to the next.

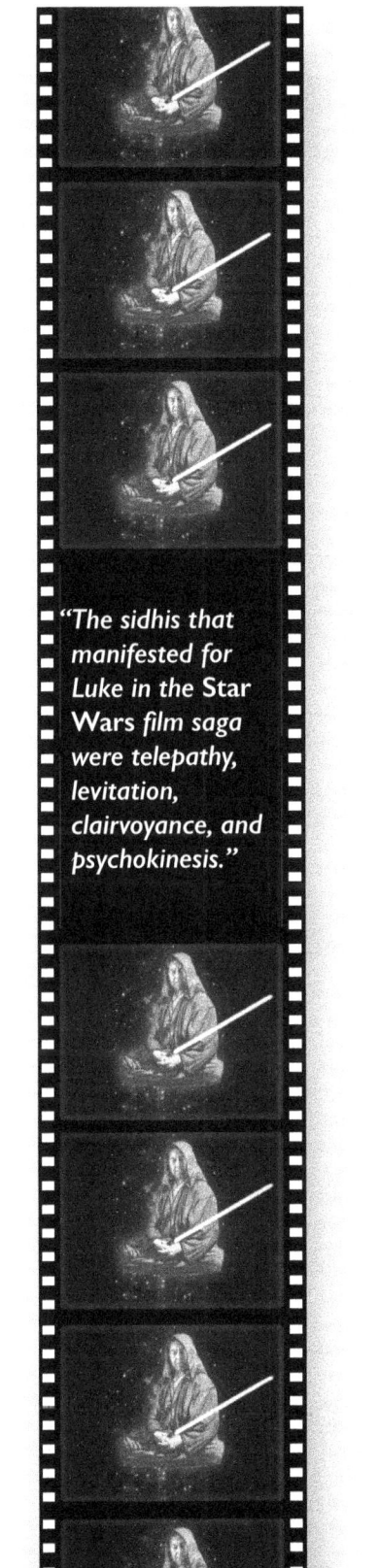

"The sidhis that manifested for Luke in the Star Wars film saga were telepathy, levitation, clairvoyance, and psychokinesis."

"In order to approach a creation as sublime as the Bhagavad-Gita with full understanding it is necessary to attune our soul to it."

— Rudolph Steiner

CHAPTER 15
HOW ANTHROPOSOPHY RESUSCITATED A DYING *STAR WARS* SCRIPT

If it weren't for Anthroposophy, the metaphysical philosophical system developed by Rudolph Steiner in the beginning of the 20th century, there might never have been a *Star Wars* movie, let alone seven others, and eventually more to come after that. This is according to Dr. Douglas Gabriel, a leading Steiner scholar affiliated with the holistic Waldorf Schools founded by the great Austrian philosopher and esoteric teacher.

The Anthroposophist wrote about a creative think tank that he led with a couple of Waldorf Institute colleagues for Marcia Lucas who, at the time, was George Lucas's wife, and a top Hollywood film editor in her own right (*Taxi Driver, American Graffiti, The Candidate*). She would go on to win an Oscar for *Star Wars*. At the time that they met, though, she had come from Hollywood for her journey to the east—specifically Michigan—to gain support from her former Anthroposophy mentor Werner Glass. The problem was that the mechanical and lifeless film script that she brought was on life support and needed archetypal and spiritual revitalization.

In a fascinating article entitled "Source of the Force: Secret Behind Star Wars Inspiration" (http://cosmicconvergence.org/?p=12888), Dr. Gabriel outlines the events by which a broken-down second script for *Star Wars* was rehabilitated and resurrected into what would eventually become perhaps the most successful franchise in cinematic history. When Mr. Glass, his mentor and the mentor of Marcia Lucas, was unable to spend any time on the project, he put Dr. Gabriel in charge.

RENAMING LUKE STARKILLER

Luke Starkiller was the name of the script's hero when George Lucas's wife brought it to her Anthroposophy colleagues. One of the first suggestions made by Dr. Gabriel was to change the character's name to one that was less negative and far more inspiring, and Skywalker certainly is both. The term "skywalker" is the name of the Chinese sun monkey king who was said to be able to walk across the sky at speeds infinitely faster than the gods, according to Professor Gabriel.

But that's not all that he and his fellows brought to the three-day script session. He found that telling the *Star Wars* story from the point of view of a pair of robots—R2D2 and C-3PO—was a big mistake, and wouldn't get anywhere near the kind of receptive response from audiences if the script were more person-oriented, and the kind of science fiction fairy tale that it would eventually evolve into. That change, fortunately, was made.

What's more, said the Anthroposophy students, the characters should be archetypal, and the struggle more of a human struggle between the higher Self and the lower. The Evil Emperor and Darth Vader embodied such negative forces—the Emperor representing the left side of the Force, which is thinking devoid of relationships, while Vader, a hybrid machine-man representing the right side, or force devoid of consciousness. Luke, they reasoned, should eventually move to the center of the force, between these two very misguided extremes.

If it weren't for the creative collaboration between the film's editor and several Waldorf Institute adherents there may never have been the famous light sabers that lit up Jedi battles. The second script that was brought to the brainstorming session featured the Jedi warriors sporting guns. Dr. Gabriel's reaction to that detail was swift and definitive: "No, no, no, no, no, no! No guns." The Jedi warrior, he put forth, has an aura "that can take anything shot at him and turn it back to the person it came from." The light saber, of course, also lends a magical element to combat that raises the film to the sci-fi fairy tale that the Waldorf teachers envisioned.

STAR WARS & THE WIZARD OF OZ

Dr. Gabriel and his Anthroposophy colleagues wanted to give Luke Skywalker a group of fellow journeyers, much like Dorothy Gale had in *The Wizard of Oz*. Like *Oz*, another classic fairy tale film, which gave the heroine friends who represented various aspects of her own soul (a

Scarecrow who symbolized the quest for consciousness and wisdom; a Tin Man who sought the compassion of a full heart; and a Lion seeking courage or spirit), the *Star Wars* script that evolved during those three days equipped its hero with similar support. The Wookie Chewbacca, for example, represented the animal in man who is in tune with Nature, but on a primitive level, inspiring Luke to raise his own consciousness above that animal vibration. The smuggler Han Solo, while clearly more rational, often responded to situations by the seat of his pants and lacked the big picture that a true hero needs. His instinctive adventurous nature—truly entrepreneurial—was invaluable to Luke on his mission. Obi-Wan Kenobi represented the spiritual part of Luke's soul and guided him toward more evolutionary choices. He did this in body when he was alive, and even in his disembodied state after his death in a battle with Darth Vader, a sacrifice that he made to ensure the escape from the Death Star by Luke and his comrades, who had just rescued Princess Leia. While Yoda was clearly Luke's spiritual master, Obi-Wan Kenobi certainly played a similar role. Lastly, there was Princess Leia, Luke's twin sister who he rescued from the Death Star, even before he was finally told by Yoda of the genetic bond that he shared with the rescued royal. Before Luke learned of the sibling connection that he shared with Leia in utero, he was quite attracted to her; after he discovered their genetic link, however, he quickly changed his tune, and said to her, "I have to find you spiritually attractive, and we must work together to defeat evil and create a new kingdom." Luke's task, therefore, involved rediscovering his lost father and sister, and restoring harmony to his society. To successfully complete such a truly Herculean mission, of course, he had to awaken his large Self, as well; a spiritual quest that his companions helped him with in many important ways. The influence of Yoda and Obi-Wan Kenobi were obvious in this metaphysical transformation of the youth, but the roles played by these other friends were also quite substantial.

MEGA $UCCESS

George and Marcia Lucas were so thrilled with the creative contributions from Marcia's Anthroposophy colleagues that they invited the spiritual team to attend a special screening of the film in Hollywood as a fundraiser for the Waldorf movement. The group in Michigan was appreciative, but declined the invitation and the trek westward. As the producing force behind this film about the Force, Lucas could certainly afford it.

Each of the eight films released so far have either won or been nominated for Academy Awards, and the total oeuvre has amassed box office grosses of nearly $6.5 billion, a truly out-of-this-galaxy financial bonanza. To date, the eight films in the *Star Wars* saga have been nominated for a whopping 24 Oscars (an average of three per film), winning nine; the movies have also won a total of three Special Achievement Awards by the Academy. The franchise has also been cited by *The Guinness Book of World Records* for the "most successful film merchandising franchise." By 2012, before the advent of the third trilogy, the total value of the franchise had been estimated at $30.7 billion. That same year, the Disney organization acquired LucasFilm for $4.06 billion.

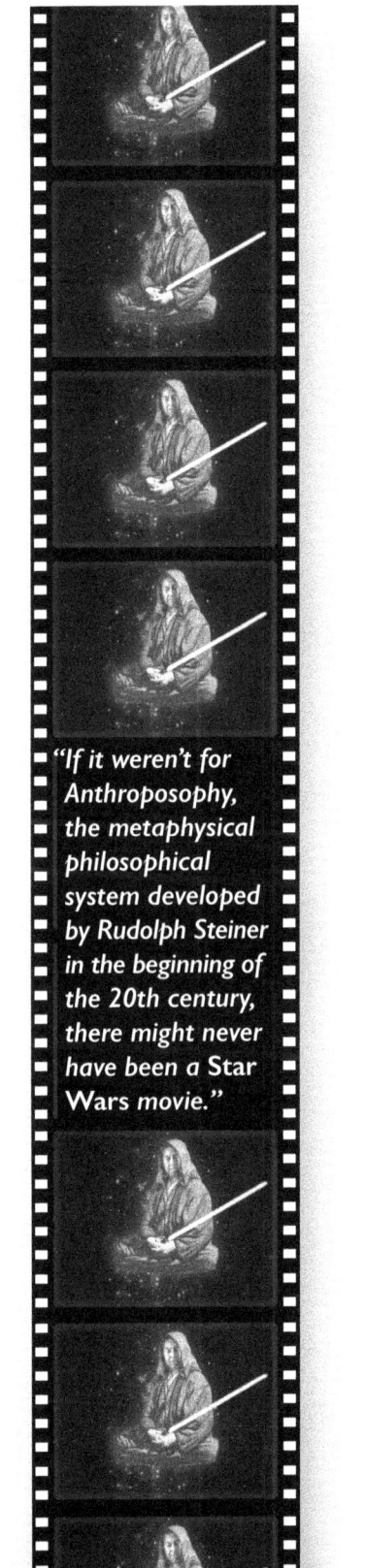

"If it weren't for Anthroposophy, the metaphysical philosophical system developed by Rudolph Steiner in the beginning of the 20th century, there might never have been a Star Wars movie."

"Little souls find their way to you, whether they're from your womb or someone else's."

— Sheryl Crow

CHAPTER 16
LUKE'S UNCONSCIOUSNESS OF HIS FAMILY: A METAPHOR FOR RECONNECTING TO YOUR SOURCE

Luke Skywalker was raised in Tatooine, by Owen and Beru Lars, his uncle and aunt. His mother Padme Amidala had died in childbirth, and he knew he had a father but he didn't know who he was, and he had no idea that he had a sister, let alone a twin who was raised to become a princess. It wasn't until Luke became a young man that he discovered that his father was Anakin Skywalker, the evil Darth Vader, a fallen Jedi who was the murdering lieutenant of the evil Emperor.

Knowing who your parents are means knowing where you come from; in other words, what your source is. So, when you don't know who your parents are, you're disconnected from your source. As we saw in chapter 2, your spiritual source is the Force itself. So Luke's unconsciousness of his familial source is a metaphor for his unconsciousness of his spiritual source.

Interestingly, as Yoda introduced Luke to his higher nature through the very deep and extensive Jedi training, the disciple learned the identity of his real father. As his hero journey unfolded, he also came to learn that he had a twin sister, the young princess who he had also taken a romantic shine to. Often, the hero journey changes your plans, and this romantic one was among them.

As we saw in chapter 2, meditation is a highly effective method for making conscious connections to your spiritual source. Thus, during Luke's Jedi training, he became conscious of his familial source, as well as conscious of his spiritual source. Luke's discovery that he has a sister—a twin, no less—and a father—even though an evil one, at that—awakens in us, as viewers in the darkened movie theater, a sense that there might be a deeper connection to our true Source awaiting us, as well. If only we could find an Obi-Wan Kenobi or a Yoda to help show us the way. Of course, in our lives, there are many such great teachers from spiritual traditions in all parts of the globe. As the saying, attributed to both the Buddha and to Theosophy, goes: "When the student is ready, the teacher appears." Are you ready?

"Luke's unconsciousness of his familial source is a metaphor for his unconsciousness of his spiritual source."

"What I told you was true from a certain point of view."
— Obi-Wan Kenobi

CHAPTER 17
SAYINGS FROM A GALAXY FAR, FAR AWAY

ANGER
"To control your anger is to be a Jedi." — Anakin Skywalker

APPEARANCES
"Judge me by my size, do you?" — Yoda

ARROGANCE
[Arrogance is] *"a flaw more and more common among the Jedi. Too sure of themselves they are. Even the older, more experienced ones."* — Yoda

ASPIRATIONS
"Be careful not to choke on your aspirations." — Darth Vader

ATTACHMENT
"Attachment is forbidden. Possession is forbidden." — Anakin Skywalker

BALANCE
"Without the Jedi there can be no balance in the Force." — Lor San Tekka

BEGINNINGS
"This is a new day, a new beginning." — Ahsoka Tano

BELIEFS
"Many of the truths that we cling to depend on our point of view."
— Obi-Wan Kenobi

"Sometimes, when you believe something to be real, it becomes real."
— Anakin Skywalker

CHANGE
"You can't stop the change." — Shmi Skywalker

CLARITY
"Clear your mind must be." — Yoda

"Mind tricks don't work on me." — Watto

COMMITMENT
"Do or do not. There is no try." — Yoda

COMPASSION
"Compassion, which I would define as unconditional love, is essential to a Jedi's life. So you might say that we are encouraged to love." — Anakin Skywalker

CONCENTRATION
"Don't center on your anxieties…keep your concentration here and now where it belongs." — Qui-Gon Jinn

"Concentrate…Feel the Force flow." — Yoda

CONSCIOUSNESS
"There is more than one sort of prison, Captain. I sense that you carry yours wherever you go." — Chirrut Inwe

COURAGE
"Never tell me the odds." — Han Solo

"One fighter with a sharp stick, with nothing left to lose, can win the day." — Lyn Erso

CRAVINGS
"Adventure. Excitement. A Jedi craves not these things." — Yoda

DARK SIDE OF THE FORCE
"The ability to destroy a planet is insignificant next to the power of the Force."
—Darth Vader

"Hard to see, the dark side is." — Yoda

"The dark side clouds everything." — Yoda

"I'll never turn to the dark side." — Luke Skywalker

[The Dark Side is] *"quicker, easier, more seductive."* — Yoda

DESPAIR
"I've traveled too far and seen too much to ignore the despair in the galaxy."
— Lor San Tekka

DESTINY
"I will fulfill our destiny." — Kylo Ren

"I should be! Someday I will be." — Anakin Skywalker

DETACHMENT
"Train yourself to let go of everything you fear to lose." — Yoda

DHARMA (PURPOSE)
"But this I am sure of. Do their duty, the Jedi will." — Yoda

DYING
"Twilight is upon me, and soon night must fall. That is the way of things…the way of the Force." — Yoda

FAMILY
"The Force is strong in my family. My father has it. I have it. My sister has it. You have that power, too." — Luke Skywalker

FEAR
"Fear is the path to the dark side." — Yoda

"The fear of loss is a path to the dark side." — Yoda

"Fear leads to anger. Anger leads to hate. Hate leads to suffering." — Yoda

FEELINGS

"Be mindful of your feelings." — Qui-Gon Jinn

"You must do what you feel is right." — Obi-Wan Kenobi

"Trust your feelings." — Obi-Wan Kenobi

"Your eyes can deceive you. Don't trust them. Stretch out with your feelings."
— Obi-Wan Kenobi

FOCUS

"Stay on target." — Gold Five

"Concentrate on the moment. Feel, don't think, use your instincts." — Qui-Gon Jinn

"Be mindful...always remember your focus determines your reality."
— Qui-Gon Jinn

FOOLISHNESS

"Who's more foolish? The fool or the fool who follows him?"
— Obi-Wan Kenobi

THE FORCE

"Remember...the Force will be with you, always." — Obi Wan Kenobi

"The force is strong with this one." — Darth Vader

"Use the force, let go." — Obi-Wan Kenobi

"You will know when you are calm, at peace. Passive. A Jedi uses the Force for knowledge and defense, never for attack." — Yoda

"For my ally is the Force, and a powerful ally it is." — Yoda

"You must feel the Force around you. Here, between you...me...the tree...the rock...everywhere! Yes, even between the land and the ship!" — Yoda

"Use the Force, Luke." — Obi-Wan Kenobi

Chapter 17—Sayings from a Galaxy Far, Far Away

"A Jedi's strength flows from the Force." — Yoda

"The Force can have a strong influence on the weak-minded." — Obi-Wan Kenobi

"A Jedi can feel the Force flowing through him." — Obi-Wan Kenobi

"That's not how the Force works." — Han Solo

"I am no Jedi, but I know the Force. It moves through and surrounds every living thing. Close your eyes…Feel it…The light…It's always been there. It will guide you. The saber. Take it." — Maz Kanata

"It [the Force] also obeys your commands." — Obi-Wan Kenobi

"I'm one with the Force. The Force is with me." — Chirrut Imwe

"Only a fully trained Jedi Knight with the Force as his ally will conquer Vader and his Emperor." — Yoda

HATE
"Let go of your hate." — Luke Skywalker

HOPE
"Hope is not lost today. It is found." — Leia

HUMILITY
"Great, kid. Don't get cocky." — Han Solo

INNOCENCE
"Truly wonderful the mind of a child is." — Yoda

INSPIRATION
"Light the place up. Make 10 men feel like 100." — Cassian Andor

INSTINCT
"Let go of your conscious self and act on instinct." — Obi-Wan Kenobi

INTUITION
"I've got a bad feeling about this." — Obi-Wan Kenobi & Han Solo

"Your eyes can deceive you. Don't trust them." — Obi-Wan Kenobi

INVINCIBILITY
"You can't win, Darth. Strike me down, and I will become more powerful than you could possibly imagine." — Obi-Wan Kenobi

"In time you will learn to trust your feelings; then you will be invincible." — Palpatine

KNOWLEDGE
"You must unlearn what you learned." — Yoda

LAUGHTER
"Laugh it up, Fuzzball." — Han Solo

LAW OF ATTRACTION
"Your focus determines your reality." — Qui-Gon Jinn

LETTING GO
"Sometimes we must let go of our pride and do what is requested of us."
— Padme Amidala

"Use the Force Luke, let go Luke... Luke trust me." — Obi-Wan Kenobi

LIGHT
"There is still light in him. I know it." — Leia

LUCK
"In my experience there is no such thing as luck." — Obi-Wan Kenobi

MIDI-CHLORIANS
"They continually speak to you, telling you the will of the Force." — Qui-Gon Jinn

MINDFULNESS
"Be mindful of the living Force." — Mace Windu

NEEDS
"Already know you that which you need." — Yoda

NOW
"Remember, concentrate on the moment. Feel, don't think, use your instincts."
— Qui-Gon Jinn

PATIENCE
"Patience you must have, my young Padawan." — Yoda

PATTERNS
"If you live long enough you see the same eyes in different people." — Maz Kanata

PLAN
"Nothing happens by accident." — Qui-Gon Jinn

POWER
"All who gain power are afraid to lose it." — Palpatine

"Why don't you use your divine influence and get us out of this?" — Han Solo

PRECOGNITION
"Careful you must be when sensing the future." — Yoda

[Anakin] *"can see things before they happen."* — Qui-Gon Jinn

PROPHECY
"If the prophecy is true, your apprentice is the only one who can bring the Force back into balance." — Mace Windu

PURPOSEFUL
"A Jedi must have the deepest commitment, the most serious mind…All his life he looked away…to the future, to the horizon. Never his mind on where he was."
— Yoda

QUESTIONS
"I never ask that question 'till after I've done it." — Han Solo

QUIETING
"When you learn to quiet your mind, you will hear them (midi-chlorians) speaking to you." — Qui-Gon Jinn

REBELLION
"Rebellions are built on hope." — Casian Andor and Jyn Erso

"Save the rebellion. Save the dream." — Saw Gerrera

REBIRTH
"Death is a natural part of life. Rejoice for those around you who transform into the Force." — Yoda

RESPONSIBILITY
"People are counting on us. The galaxy is counting on us." — Han Solo

REUNITING
"We'll see each other again. I believe that." — Rey

SEEKING
"The belonging you seek is not behind you…it is ahead." — Maz Kanata

SELF
"It is the name of your true Self; you have only forgotten." — Luke Skywalker

SELF-SUFFICIENCY
"I think I can handle myself." — Rey

SHARING
"Always pass on what you have learned." — Yoda

SPEECH
"Don't talk that way. You have a power I–I don't understand and could never have."
— Princess Leia

TEACHER
"You need a teacher. I can show you the ways of the Force." — Kylo Ren

THOUGHTS
"Be mindful of your thoughts; they will betray you." — Obi-Wan Kenobi

TIME
"Difficult to see. Always in motion is the future." — Yoda

Chapter 17—Sayings from a Galaxy Far, Far Away

TRAINING
"If you end your training now—if you choose the quick and easy path, as Vader did—you will become an agent of evil." — Yoda

"I am ready to face the trials." — Obi-Wan Kenobi

TRUST
"Trust the Force." — Lyra Erso

WAR
"Wars not make one great." — Yoda

WOMEN
"Women always figure out the truth. Always." — Han Solo

"Assume a virtue if you have it not."
— William Shakespeare, *Hamlet*

CHAPTER 18
INTRODUCTION: AFFIRMING YOUR CALL TO THE ADVENTURE OF PEACEFUL JEDI MIND TRAINING

Removing unconscious resistance to the success of your hero journey as a peaceful Jedi is vital, and a powerful way to accomplish this is by rewiring your Unconscious mind. An excellent way to do that is through the technique of affirmations, and the best way of using affirmations is with the three-part holistic process that I'll be describing below.

The Jedi Mind Training Affirmation Process

At the top of your page in the left margin write the affirmation as 1A; below that in the left margin, write the response that it elicits from your lower self as 1B; and below that in the left margin, create a new affirmation from your higher Self that represents a positive antithesis of the negative response that you just wrote, and call that 1C.

The "A" step is the affirmation, a kind of seed that you plant in the soil of your consciousness that you wish to make your reality. The "B" step is the negative response in your Unconscious that blocks that affirmation from becoming your reality. The "C" step is the new affirmation from your higher Self, which is your connection to the Force at the depths of your being. The purpose of the "C" affirmation is to enlighten the smaller part of your mind that had entertained that limited response in the first place. It's a customized message that your higher Self is giving to your lower self.

For purposes of illustration, let's work with the following affirmation, one of my favorites for the inner journey of a Jedi in training:

"I can align with the Force."

Begin by writing it as 1A. Then, below that, as 1B, write the negative thought that arises in your mind in response to this affirmation. There will likely be many such thoughts that arise, and many of them frequently take the form of doubt, worry, fear, anger, and so on—seeds that can lead one to the dark side. Some of these negative emotions are a residue of any alignment you may have had with the dark side of the Force. (In Greek mythology there is a god named Momus whose principal activity was mockery and faultfinding. It appears as if this god has been internalized into the inner chatter in the minds of virtually every human being alive today.) A possible negative response to this affirmation might be written in the following way:

"I don't know how to align with the Force."

The beauty of this process accepts, without any kind of judgment whatsoever, in the second step, the negativity that prevents the affirmation from becoming your reality. Writing the response, releases the resistance from your being.

Then, below that, write a new affirmation, as 1C, to specifically treat this resistance. A good one in this case is:

"I'm willing to see that the Force is within me as my deepest nature, so becoming aligned with it simply means being conscious of my true nature."

Write this "A" affirmation in this three-part process for 10 minutes a day until its truth starts to manifest in your daily life. What follows this introduction are many dozens of other affirmations that you can also use to speed up and make smooth your inner transformation into a peaceful Jedi in tune with the living Force. My recommendation is to work on only one at a time for at least the space of a week.

Journey on! May the Force not only be with you, but may you consciously realize that it has always been with you and always will be. And that's because It is you—or better yet, you are It.

"Removing unconscious resistance to the success of your hero journey as a peaceful Jedi is vital, and a powerful way to accomplish this is by rewiring your Unconscious mind."

"As he thinketh in his heart, so is he."

— Proverbs 23:7

CHAPTER 19
JEDI MIND TRAINING: AFFIRMATIONS FOR ALIGNING WITH THE FORCE

A

ACTION
I always act in ways that are harmonious to the Force, so that I may become aligned with It.

I act with great confidence at all times.

My actions inspire others and bring out the very best in others.

ADVENTURE
My life is an unfolding and exciting adventure as a peaceful Jedi.

I embrace adventures of all kinds.

My adventures inspire others.

I was born to succeed at the supreme adventure—becoming one with the Force.

ALIGNMENT
Aligning with the Force is natural.

Aligning with the Force is effortless because the Force is my nature.

I can align with the Force.

I am now aligned with the Force.

I am always in alignment with the Force.

The more I am aligned with the Force, the more support I receive from It, and from everything in the Universe.

My alignment with the Force inspires all those who know me.

My alignment with the Force brings me success in life.

My alignment with the Force brings me joy and exhilaration in life.

APPEARANCES
I always see beyond appearances to the heart of things.

ASPIRATIONS
I aspire to the highest things in life.

My aspirations are supported by my deep connection to the Force.

ATTACHMENT
I let go of attachments to people.

I let go of attachments to the things of my life.

B

BALANCE
I stay balanced in my life.

BEING
My inner Being is my connection to the Force.

When I can simply Be, I am in tune with the Force.

Chapter 19—Jedi Mind Training: Affirmations for Aligning with the Force

BELIEFS

My beliefs are shaped by my connection to the Force.

I'm willing to let go of old beliefs that don't serve me.

BLISS

I'm now willing to enjoy the bliss of the Force at the depths of my being.

The bliss of the Force fills me with enthusiasm and excitement about being alive.

Bliss is the nature of the Force and my nature, as well.

My experience of bliss inspires others.

BOUNDARIES

I recognize when my boundaries are invaded, especially by those who work with the dark side of the Force.

It's safe to defend my boundaries from anyone who would invade them.

I naturally and easily defend my boundaries against anyone who would invade them.

I can defend my boundaries in a peaceful manner.

It's all right with me if others are uncomfortable when I defend my boundaries.

It's all right with me if I am uncomfortable when I defend my boundaries.

I can naturally defend the boundaries of others when they are invaded.

C

CALMNESS

Being calm enables me to more easily connect to the Force.

Calmness is my true nature.

I can stay calm in any situation.

CHALLENGES
I welcome challenges.

Challenges bring out the best in me.

My mind stays clear when others are confused by the challenges that have arisen.

CLAIRAUDIENCE
The natural ability to be clairaudient has been asleep in me for a very long time.

I'm willing to awaken the natural ability to be clairaudient.

Clairaudience is waking up as a conscious skill in my life.

It's perfectly natural to have clairaudience functioning in my life.

CLAIRVOYANCE
The natural ability to be clairvoyant has been asleep in me for a very long time.

I'm willing to awaken the natural ability to be clairvoyant.

Clairvoyance is waking up as a conscious skill in my life.

It's perfectly natural to have clairvoyance functioning in my life.

CLARITY
My connection to the Force brings me great clarity of mind.

COMMITTMENT
I give up trying, and commit to accomplishing my objectives in life.

I'm so committed to my growth and success that my decisive and powerful actions now surprise others, sometimes even myself.

I'm so committed to my success, that I move swiftly into action.

COMMUNICATION
My connection to the Force enables me to communicate clearly.

My communications flow from the Force

Communications flow smoothly and honestly in my family.

COMPASSION
I have compassion for all living beings.

I have compassion for myself.

My connection to the Force awakens my compassion, even for those who serve Its dark side.

The Force has compassion for me.

CONCENTRATION
My connection to the Force keeps my mind concentrated in the present moment.

I have great strength of mind to concentrate for long periods of time.

CONSCIOUSNESS
My consciousness is connected to the Force.

My consciousness expands the more connected I am with the Force.

My consciousness inspires others.

COURAGE
I have more than enough courage to do the things that challenge me.

It's natural to be courageous.

My courage continuously surprises me.

My courage inspires others.

I can manifest bravery even when I'm frightened.

I can do the things that scare me, and I can do them extremely well.

I am braver than I ever knew I was.

My courage surfaces and expresses itself when I am defending righteousness.

D

THE DARK SIDE OF THE FORCE
I resist the temptations of the dark side of the Force now and forever.

I am impervious to the presence of the dark side of the Force in others.

I avoid those who are aligned with the dark side of the Force.

I let go of all attachments I may ever have had with the dark side of the Force.

DECISIVENESS
My clarity of mind enables me to be highly decisive.

My decisions are always in tune with the Force.

DOUBT
I now let go of all my doubts.

Doubting is a thing of my past.

Certainty strengthens me in everything that I do.

My certainty certainly inspires others.

I never doubt my heroic nature anymore.

DYING

I accept the process of dying when it occurs.

I relax into the process of dying when my time comes.

I understand death as a transition into a bigger afterlife.

E

EFFORTLESSNESS

The more connected I am to the Force the more effortless is my life.

Fulfilling my desires occurs effortlessly.

ENDURANCE

My alignment with the Force inspires me to persevere and endure all challenges.

I have great stamina.

ENLIGHTENMENT

When I live fully in alignment with the Force I enjoy the freedom of Enlightenment.

My Enlightenment continually inspires others to pursue their spiritual quest for Enlightenment.

ENTHUSIASM

My connection to the Force blesses me with natural enthusiasm that aids me in my spiritual development.

My enthusiasm attracts others to me.

My enthusiasm draws opportunities to me.

My enthusiasm prospers me.

F

FAMILY
I always see the best in the people in my family, even when others don't.

I love everyone in my family, despite their imperfections.

There is harmony in my family.

FEAR
I never let fear stop me from doing what's right.

FEELINGS
My connection to the Force keeps me well connected to my feelings, as well.

I always trust my feelings.

FOCUS
I always stay focused on what's most important.

It's easy for me to stay focused.

THE FORCE
The Force breathes for me.

The Force beats the heart in my chest.

The Force digests the food that I eat.

The Force gets me up in the morning.

The Force puts me to sleep at night.

The Force is within me and outside of me at all times.

The Force supports my desires.

I serve the will of the Force.

Chapter 19—Jedi Mind Training: Affirmations for Aligning with the Force

The Force is a force for good in this world.

The Force and I are one.

FORGIVENESS
I now forgive myself completely.

I now forgive my father completely, no matter whatever terrible things he did to me.

I now forgive my mother completely, no matter whatever terrible things she did to me.

I forgive those aligned with the dark side of the Force.

Forgiveness makes me more heroic.

Forgiveness makes me a greater Jedi for peace.

G

GALAXY
The galaxy that I live in is my home.

I am at home wherever I am in the galaxy.

GRACE
My constant connection to the Force fills my life with grace.

My experience of grace inspires others to live a more spiritual and graceful life.

GRATITUDE
I am forever grateful to the Force for blessing my life in so many countless ways.

The more grateful I am for my connection to the Force, the more connected I am to be grateful for.

GUIDANCE
I attract guidance from many sources both within me and outside of me.

I am forever guided by Infinite Intelligence and Infinite Love, both of which are aspects of the Force.

My guides are always there to lead me to my highest Good, and deepen my connection to the Force.

GURU
My guru teaches me the wisdom of Yoga in much the same way that Yoda taught the wisdom of the Jedis.

H

HAPPINESS
My happiness deepens as my connection to the Force deepens.

My happiness inspires others to connect more deeply to the Force.

My happiness inspires happiness in others.

HEALING
I can heal from injuries quickly.

My connection to the Force strengthens my immune system.

HEALTH
I remain healthy at all times.

HEART
My heart grows in life as my connection to the Force grows.

My love of the Force purifies my heart.

The more I love the Force, the more I love everyone in my life.

HERO/HEROINE
I am a hero (heroine).

It's safe to be a hero (heroine).

My connection to the Force makes me capable of greater heroism than I ever thought possible.

My heroism inspires heroism in others.

HUMILITY
My connection to the Force keeps me humble.

My connection to the Force makes me realize that I'm nobody special.

I

INFINITY
My connection to the Force reveals to me the infinite nature of my consciousness.

My connection to the Force brings me infinite possibilities in my life.

My connection to the Force brings me infinite possibilities in my career.

INFLUENCE
I can influence the minds of others for good.

My connection to the Force enables me to influence the minds of others.

INNOCENCE
My innocence inspires innocence in others.

My innocence attracts support from my friends and the Force.

My innocence disarms negative forces in my life that may arise from those who are in allegiance to the dark side of the Force.

INSPIRATION
My connection to the Force inspires others.

It's natural for me to be an inspiration for others to connect to the Force.

The inspiration that I draw from the Force makes me stronger and more peaceful.

INSTINCTS
My connection to the Force enables my instincts to be easy to trust and follow.

I always feel in my gut the right thing to do to be in tune with the Force.

Since my instincts always guide me properly, I naturally act upon them.

My instincts protect me.

INSTRUMENT
I am an instrument through which the Force is made manifest in the world.

INTUITION
The more connected I am to the Force, the more access I have to my intuition.

My intuition is the Force talking to me between my thoughts.

I know things without having to be told in the usual ways.

My highly developed intuitive sense is a great blessing from the Force.

My intuition prospers me.

J

JEDI
I can be a kind of peaceful Jedi.

As a peaceful Jedi, I spread harmony in my life.

I am a peaceful Jedi, staying connected to the light side of the Force.

JOURNEY
My life is a journey back to my true home of spiritual peace.

Chapter 19—Jedi Mind Training: Affirmations for Aligning with the Force 125

I enjoy being on a journey to wholeness.

My hero journey is an exciting adventure.

The speed of my journey intensifies greatly when I heed the call to adventure.

I now hear the call to adventure in life and welcome it.

My inner journey begins and ends at my true Source, my higher Self, where I am one with the Force.

My journey ends in fulfillment.

My inner Jedi journey inspires others to embark on their inner journeys, as well.

JUSTICE
I am committed to living in a just world.

I work to create justice in my world.

K

KARMA
I now let myself create positive karma through my positive thinking, speech, and behavior.

I handle the return of my negative karma with grace and peace.

KNOWLEDGE
My knowledge of the Force helps me understand the experiences that I have on my journey.

I know how to contact the Force.

I know how to live in tune with the Force.

My connection to the Force provides me with knowledge of many subtle things.

L

LAUGHTER
My connection to the Force enables me to laugh a lot.

My laughter enriches the hearts of others.

LAW OF ATTRACTION
I understand that my thoughts and speech help shape the reality that I live in.

The more I expand my belief systems the larger my life becomes.

LEADERSHIP
My connection to the Force is so strong that I naturally lead others in my career.

My connection to the Force makes me a natural born leader in many areas of my life.

LETTING GO
I now let go of everything that doesn't serve me.

I now let go of the dark side of my nature.

LEVITATION
The natural ability to levitate has been asleep in me for a very long time.

I am willing to awaken the natural ability to levitate.

Levitation is waking up as a conscious skill in my life.

LIGHT
My connection to the Force awakens the inner Light in me.

I always live in the Light.

THE LIGHT SIDE OF THE FORCE
I align myself with the light side of the Force.

I love everything about the light side of the Force.

I recognize others who are aligned with the light side of the Force.

The light side of the Force is always there for me.

LOVE
Love is the answer to any problem on my journey.

Love grows in me daily.

Love adds joy to my life and to the lives of others.

When I love others, the Force is strong in me.

My love for others inspires others to love the people in their lives more deeply.

LUCK
My connection to the Force enables me to enjoy good fortune and luck.

M

MEDIATION
My connection to the Force enables me to mediate disputes of others with grace and skill.

MEDITATION
I use meditation as a way to connect to the Force.

I let the Force guide my meditations.

Meditation is an effortless process that's guided by the Force to help me become conscious of It.

MIND

My mind's connection to the Infinite Intelligence of the Force is more than enough to always guide me in proper directions in my personal life and in my career.

My mind's connection to the Force helps me find all the answers that I ever need.

My mind is always clear.

My mind inspires others.

My mind always leads me to right decisions.

MINDFULNESS

I do everything in life with mindfulness.

MIRACLES

Miracles grow in my life as I grow in my connection to the Force.

Miracles are natural when I'm in tune with the Force.

N

NEEDS

My needs are fulfilled by the Force as they arise.

NOW

The more connected I am to the Force, the more I live in the Now moment.

The Now moment is infinite in its richness and depth.

I delight in living from the infinite depths of the Now moment.

O

OBSTACLES

I can surmount any obstacle that befalls my path.

Obstacles are no barriers to my evolution as a Jedi for peace.

P

PATH
The Path that I walk as a Jedi for peace is smooth, easy and joyful.

When breakdowns arise on my Path, I have the insight, the patience, and the courage to persevere for breakthroughs.

As I walk my Path as a Jedi for peace, I attract companions, who help me along the way.

My way is the right way.

My Path is a pleasure to walk.

PATIENCE
I have great patience.

My understanding and connection to the Force enables me to have patience for things to take place in their time.

PEACE
I can be at peace in any dangerous situation on my journey.

Peace is my true nature.

Being at peace enables me to always recognize the light side of the Force.

I am in the process of living in peace on an ongoing basis.

My journey is one of unfolding peace.

I am an instrument through which peace is established in the galaxy.

My peace attracts support from the Force.

I am a Jedi messenger of peace.

My peace helps to awaken peace in others, and inspires them to be instruments of peace, as well.

PLAN
I can live spontaneously from the Force and still plan things strategically.

I'm flexible enough to change my plans when the Force has other plans.

POWERS
I'm capable of awakening sleeping superhuman powers within me.

Superhuman powers are now awakening within me.

I use my superhuman powers only for the good of all concerned.

PROSPERITY
I choose to use the gifts that the Force has bestowed upon me in my career.

Utilizing the gifts and talents that the Force has bestowed upon me leads me to a smooth career, and prosperity in life.

The Force prospers me.

My prosperity inspires others.

PRECOGNITION
I'm willing to allow my sleeping powers of precognition to awaken now.

I trust my ability to know things before they happen.

PSYCHOKINESIS
The ability to move objects with the mind is a natural gift bestowed upon everyone in the galaxy, including me.

I'm willing to embrace my gift of psychokinesis.

Psychokinesis is a natural part of my daily life.

PURPOSE
It's my purpose to live from the light side of the Force.

It's my purpose to bring harmony to my world.

It's my purpose to defend the world from those who live from the dark side of the Force.

Q

QUEST
My connection to the Force enables me to succeed in my spiritual quest.

The success of my spiritual quest inspires others to embark on their spiritual quests, as well.

QUIETNESS
I take time to enjoy mental quietness a couple of times each day.

The more I quiet my mind, the clearer I hear the will of the Force.

QUIXOTIC
My connection to the Force enables me to succeed in even my most quixotic of undertakings.

R

REBIRTH
My connection to the Force enables me to enjoy a rebirth of Spirit in my life.

I now enjoy a rebirth of Spirit.

RESPONSIBILITY
My connection to the Force enables me to be responsible in my life.

I handle increasing responsibility with increasing grace.

REUNITING

I enjoy reuniting with those with whom I may be temporarily disconnected.

I enjoy reuniting with those with whom my relationship has become lost.

ROBOTS

Robots are there to help make my daily life much easier.

Robots are my friends.

S

SELF

Home is where my higher Self is, and my higher Self is my connection to the Force at the depths of my being.

My higher Self is a source of great fulfillment.

SELF-SUFFICIENCY

My connection to the Force allows me to rely on my self with great confidence.

SERENITY

Serenity expands in me as the Force expands in my consciousness.

SHADOW

I no longer need to suppress my Shadow just to acknowledge it.

When I incorporate my Shadow, it ceases to frighten me, and enables me to resist the lures of the dark side of the Force.

My Shadow no longer frustrates me or sabotages my desires.

I am at peace with my Shadow. Any evil within me melts away in the face of my purity.

SHARING

I enjoy sharing things with others.

I enjoy sharing my feelings with others.

I enjoy sharing my life with others.

SPEAKING
I speak harmoniously to everyone so that my alignment with the Force can be maintained.

My speech is pleasing to the Force, and everyone I speak with.

STAMINA
I have the stamina to withstand difficult and long challenges.

My stamina continues to grow.

SUPPORT OF THE FORCE
The more connected I am to the light side of the Force, the more It supports me.

The Force supports my every undertaking.

T

TEACHER
I respect my teacher completely.

I follow the guidance of my teacher.

TEACHINGS
I faithfully follow the teachings that I've been blessed to have received.

TELEPATHY
I now awaken my telepathic powers that once were asleep.

I am comfortable with my telepathic abilities.

THOUGHTS
I realize that my thoughts help create my reality.

TIME
My connection to the Force enables me to respect my time and the time of others.

TIMELESSNESS
My connection to the Force enables me to enjoy timelessness in each moment of time.

TRAINING
I practice the lessons of my training daily.

TRANSCENDENTAL
I contact the Force at the transcendental level of my Being.

I can live from the transcendental level of my Being.

TRUST
I trust all people unless I've been shown that they're not trustworthy.

TRYING
I let go of trying, and commit to doing and accomplishing.

U

UNDERSTANDING
My connection to the Force enables me to understand Reality.

UNDERTAKING
My connection to the Force affords me success in my undertakings.

V

VISUALIZATION
I visualize my journey going smoothly.

I visualize myself gaining the support of the Force.

I visualize myself at peace in my eternal Self, and one with the Force.

W

WARRIOR
I am a warrior for peace.

I use my inner strength to fight for justice in life.

I am a successful warrior for justice and peace.

WISDOM
Wisdom grows in me as I live in increasing alignment with the Force.

I delight in the wisdom of living in tune with the light side of the Force.

WORK
When I do the work that the Force has given me to do, the world is enriched and so am I, as money flows to me quickly and abundantly.

My work is part of how I express my higher nature, and my connection to the Force.

I delight in doing the work that I'm here to do.

Y

YOGA
My practice of Yoga helps me connect to the Force.

YOUTHFUL
The more I am young at heart, the more connected I am to the Force.

Z

ZEAL
I have a zeal for living in tune with the Force.

ZEST
My zest for life grows as my connection to the Force intensifies.

"Religion controls inner space; inner space controls outer space."
—Zsuzsanna Budapest, Author,
The Goddess in the Office: A Personal Energy Guide for the Spiritual Warrior at Work

CHAPTER 20
EPILOGUE: FINAL THOUGHTS FROM OUR GALAXY CLOSE, CLOSE TO YOU

For many Gen Xers weaned on Atari's Pac-Man, who were wielding joysticks long before they were lifting beer cans or weights, and for Millenials who were controlling a steering wheel-shaped device to play Wii games before they had their hands on a steering wheel to drive their own cars, the *Star Wars* saga might be enjoyed mostly as an intergalactic action adventure series. But for those of the Me Generation who were waking up spiritually during the '60s through the aid of great gurus from the East and the transformative mantras, yantras, and tantras that they taught, George Lucas's outer space adventure is also an *inner* space adventure.

While millions of fans have been thrilled by watching the Millennial Falcon hurtle through space at hyper speed and shooting enemy aircraft out of the skies with extraordinary high tech weaponry, many Baby Boomers are equally dazzled by the spiritual wizardry of Yoda, Obi-Wan Kenobi, and Luke Skywalker, among others. The filmmaker has awakened the Me Generation, dazzled the Wii generation, and, in his heroic Luke Skywalker, has shown how life isn't about just inner development for selfish purposes, but inner development to save the world. Luke was enamored of his Jedi training, but he never let it be just about waking up great latent powers; it was about using these inner gifts and his outer weapons to destroy an evil Empire and save the world for right-living, good-hearted human beings and the imaginative species, which inhabit the Lucas universe.

The filmmaker has most clearly succeeded in reaching the Comic-

Con comic book fan who's mesmerized by high-powered, high tech battles; he has also inspired the meditator and serious Yoga student who is more drawn to the inner Light than the light saber. While most every filmgoer has enjoyed the hum of the light saber that Jedis wield, meditators enjoy it on another level, recognizing the similar vibration and hum that their mantras yield when they wield them in their spiritual practices.

It has been the purpose of *"Star Wars" Yoga, the Force, and You* to lift the conversation around *Star Wars* to star *peace*, if I can coin such a term. This book has chosen to focus on the spiritual and mythological influences at work on the creative consciousness of George Lucas, tracing the connection of Yoda to Yoga, of Luke Skywalker to Luke's account of Jesus in the *New Testament*, and of the marvelous powers manifested by Jedi knights to those of superheroes and the advanced yogis throughout history who've awakened their latest abilities through the study of the great Yogi Patanjali's *Yoga Sutras*.

We've seen how Luke Skywalker, like Arjuna of the *Bhagavad Gita* fame, had to do battle with his own flesh and blood. We've learned how both of these heroes underwent a spiritual training (by Yoda and Krishna, respectively), that incorporated a thorough intellectual understanding of Reality coupled with a direct inner spiritual experience of that Reality; the pair becoming the foundation for plunging into the outer adventure of doing battle with evil forces. As we saw in chapter 4, "Yoda Yoga," Krishna taught Arjuna to "be without the three gunas;" in other words, to simply Be. Then he told him to fight evil. Once established in Yoga, the general was to engage in action, in accordance with his dharma, which was to defend his people. Yoda taught Luke that he would have inner knowledge of the Force when "you are calm, at peace." Then, from that inner foundation, he was told to engage in action, in accordance with *his* dharma, to fight the evil Emperor and defend righteousness. Luke, after all, was the son of the man who had the highest midi-chorian concentration of anyone anywhere ever in the galaxy. Who else would be strong enough in the Force to take on such a military challenge?

For some, *Star Wars* is partly a quasi-Freudian tale of a son who is forced to kill an evil father; the youth's spiritual teachers said quite unequivocally that he must destroy this fallen former wunderkind who was prophesied to bring balance to the Force until he turned to the dark side. And yet the boy could only see the good in this Satanic evil doer, who slaughtered Jedi masters and students mercilessly. We saw how, in so doing, the son miraculously awakened the light in the father, who did one great heroic and good thing before dying. In chapter 8, "The Gospel of Luke (Skywalker): Jesus & the Jedis," we saw how this profound forgiveness by Luke paralleled the compassionate forgiveness that another Luke recounted about someone named Jesus in the *New Testament*.

We also saw how George Lucas took an inner journey to the East to create the saga's spiritual glue—the Force—that bears striking similarities to the Tao of China espoused so eloquently by the great sage Lao Tzu in the *Tao Te Ching* some twenty-five hundreds years ago (chapter 6, "The Force & the Tao"). Both the Tao and the Force contain a light side and a dark side, and adherents of both developed martial arts trainings based upon these deep spiritual realities, whether they were referred to by others as samurais or Jedis.

The great popularity of the teachings of the Buddha, who lived in a time far, far away, is helping bijou ticket holders of today come to appreciate the inner wisdom of the letting go of control, of thought, and of will that Luke's teachers instructed him to do. This letting go can help them, like it helped their hero Luke, simply let things be and destroy whatever Death Stars that might terrorize them in their daily lives (chapter 5, "The Buddha & Yoda").

We saw how the *Star Wars* creator took a journey through time to continents far, far away, modeling his Jedi knights after knights of the Middle Ages in Europe and monks in China nearly a millennium before that (chapter 10, "Jedi Knights & the Round Table: *Star Wars*, Camelot, & the Middle Ages"). We also saw how he borrowed from ancient myths from far away lands, aided in part by the great mythology master, Joseph Campbell, who the filmmaker referred to as "my Yoda" (chapter 11, "A New Mythos from a Galaxy Far, Far Away").

These are just some of the insights that we can glean from this great filmmaker's remarkable tale now entering its fifth decade. I'm not prescient enough to know where George Lucas will finally take this story. We've seen generations of heroes and villains, so there's no telling how far into the future he might take us. But there are two things that I am fairly certain of. One is that there will be newer adventures involving light saber battles and wondrous weapons performing all manner of dramatic destructions. And the other is that there will be newer spiritual insights dawning in the consciousness of *Star Wars* heroes that will help them do remarkable things. I know this because the Force is clearly with George Lucas, and the Force has much that It wishes to teach him, much that It wishes to teach you and me, much that It wishes us to be, and much that It wishes us to share in the world.

May the Force always be with you.

ABOUT THE AUTHOR

Cary Bayer has led seminars in North America and Europe on Prosperity, Meditation, Relationships, Purpose, Communications, Procrastination, Superheroes, *Star Wars*, *The Wizard of Oz*, and the Healing Power of Laughter, among other topics. He also coaches people and businesses—in person and by phone—to create ongoing breakthroughs. The experience of teaching Transcendental Meditation to hundreds of people from the time he was 20 through 2009, coupled with training dozens of its teachers, inspired Cary to develop Higher Self Healing Meditation in 2010. It's a new meditation for a new age, that's as easy and effective as TM at a third of the price.

A full-time Life Coach since 2001, he's worked with Oscar-winners Alan Arkin (*Little Miss Sunshine*) and Pietro Scalia (*JFK*, *Black Hawk Down*), Emmy-winners David Steinberg (*Academy Awards* presentations) and Judy Henderson (*Homeland*), and Quality Inns.

He appears often on television and radio, and has authored 15 full-length books, including *Prosperity Aerobics*; *Relationships 101*; *Conscious Communication*; *40 Days to a Happy Life*; *Higher Self Meditations*; *How to Overcome Procrastination Now*; *A Course in* Money *Miracles*; and *The Yoga of Entertainment*; as well as a trilogy for massage therapists—*Think and Grow a Rich Massage Business*; *Market and Grow a Rich Massage Business*; and *Communicate and Grow a Rich Massage Business*. He also has created more than a dozen CDs and DVDs.

He has written for *New Age*, *Playboy*, New York's *Daily News*, and the *San Francisco Chronicle*, and writes "Life 101," a syndicated column for wellness publications throughout the U.S. He also writes a coaching column for *Massage Today* nationally, and for massage publications in 14 states, and is a frequent contributor to *Massage* Magazine.

His eclectic influences include Maharishi Mahesh Yogi, Alan Watts, C.G. Jung, Walt Whitman, Herman Hesse, Groucho and Harpo Marx, Superman, Batman, and Zorro.

A Summa Cum Laude graduate from SUNY-Buffalo in English, Cary has an M.A. in Interdisciplinary Studies from Maharishi International University. He resides with his wife Barbara on the ocean in Hillsboro Beach, FL, and in the mountains of legendary Woodstock, NY.

ADDITIONAL READING

Achpal, Henna, "Buddhist Lessons *from* Star Wars," The Buddhist Channel, http://buddhistchannel.tv/index.php?id=12,13039,0,0,1,0#.WH0lcSMrK8V, December 12, 2016.

Anker, Roy, *Catching Light: Looking for God in the Movies*, William B. Eerdmans Publishing Co., Grand Rapids, MI, 2004

Anonymous Blogger,"Yoga and Yoda," beliefnet, http://www.beliefnet.com/entertainment/movies/2005/05/yoda-and-yoga.aspx#. 2005

Anonymous Blogger, "Zen and the Art of Being a Jedi," Mind Power News, http://www.mindpowernews.com/ZenJedi.htm

Bortolin, Matthew, *The Dharma of Star Wars*, Wisdom Publications, Somerville, MA, 2015

Brenion, Frederick, "Jedi-Shinsku: The Buddhist Heart of Star Wars," http://www.livingdharma.org/Real.World.Buddhism/StarWars-Brenion.html

Brennan, Kristen, "Star Wars Origins," http://www.moongadget.com/origins/myth.html, 2006

Decker, Kevin and Eberl, Jason, Editors, *Star Wars and Philosophy: More Powerful than you can Possibly Imagine*, Open Court, Chicago, IL, 2005

Derisz, Ricky, *From A Religion, Far, Far Away: How Eastern Spirituality And '60s Counterculture Inspired The Force In 'Star Wars'*, https://moviepilot.com/p/star-wars-real-life-inspiration-the-force/4114637, November 12, 2016

Dockins, Justin, *The Tao of the Force: Living the Wisdom of Lao Tzu and Yoda*, CreateSpace Independent Publishing for the Web, 2015

Gabriel, Douglas, "Source of the Force: Secret Behind Star Wars Inspiration," http://cosmicconvergence.org/?p=12888, Cosmic Convergence, 2016

Grimes, Caleb, *Star Wars Jesus: A Spiritual Commentary on the Reality of the Force*, WinePress Publishing, Enumclaw, WA, 2007

Hamilton, Jason, "Star Wars in Mythology: The Shadow" http://www.starwars.com/news/star-wars-in-mythology-the-shadow, 2015

Konleczny, Peter, "Star Wars and the Middle Ages," http://www.medievalists.net/2014/03/star-wars-middle-ages/, 2014.

Kreger, D.W., *The Tao of Yoda: Based Upon the Tao Te Ching, by Lao Tzu*, Windham Everitt Publishing, Palmdale, CA, 2012

Langley, Travis, & Goldman, Carrie, *Star Wars Psychology: Dark Side of the Mind*, Sterling Publishing, New York, NY, 2015

McDowell, John, *The Gospel According to Star Wars: Faith, Hope, and the Force*, Westminster John Knox Press, Louisville, KY, 2007

Moyers, Bill, "Of Myth and Men," *Time* magazine, April 18, 1999.

Pattberg, Thorsten, "Star Wars is Chinese Taoism," The East-West Dichotomy, http://www.east-west-dichotomy.com/star-wars-is-chinese-taoism/, December 16, 2015.

Perez, Daniel, "From Jediism to Judaism: Star Wars as Jewish Allegory," http://www.aish.com/j/as/From-Jediism-to-Judaism-Star-Wars-as-Jewish-Allegory.html

Porter, John, *The Tao of Star Wars*, Humanics Trade Group Publication, Atlanta, GA, 2003

Rogovoy, Seth, "The Secret Jewish History of Star Wars," http://forward.com/culture/327265/the-secret-jewish-history-of-star-wars/. December 16, 2015.

Staub, Dick, *Christian Wisdom of the Jedi Masters*, John Wiley & Sons, San Francisco, CA, 2005

Yogananda, Paramahansa, *God Talks with Arjuna: The Bhagavad Gita*, Self-Realization Fellowship, Los Angeles, CA, 1995

Yogi, Maharishi Mahesh, *On the Bhagavad Gita: A New Translation and Commentary*, Penguin Books, London, England, 1970

Calling All Producers:
Cary Bayer's Intro & Full-Day Workshops

Producers are needed to help Cary Bayer bring his teaching everywhere. As producer, you take an intro or full-day class for free. You also make money by doing work you love, receiving 40 percent of the seminar's gross revenues. You also bring breakthroughs to friends, family and community, enhancing their lives and yours as a result. Lastly, you learn to innocently A) present yourself to the world, B) ask for money and C) sell more effectively. The workshops below are presented in Cary's inimitable playful style that enables students to quickly break through previously held blocks and limitations by relaxing enough to see their situations from a much broader perspective. For full descriptions of classes, go to http://carybayer.com/workshops.html

Categories
1. Prosperity
2. Purpose & Personal Power
3. Relationships & Communication
4. Yoga & Meditation
5. Pop Culture & Higher Consciousness
6. Creativity
7. Inner Child, Happiness, & Laughter
8. Literature, & Religion
9. Seasonal
10. Business Training for Healers
11. Stress Management

1. **Prosperity:** A. "The Secret of Money: How to use the Law of Attraction for Financial Health & Wealth," B. "Spirit & Money: Prospering by Doing what You Love," C. "A Course in Money Miracles," D. "How to Discover & Use your Money Mantra"

2. **Purpose & Personal Power:** A. "How to Discover & Live Your Purpose," B. "How to Overcome Procrastination Now,"

C. "Thoughtmail™: Mastering the Inner Technology for Happiness & Success," D. "Love Trumps Hate: Tools for Spiritual & Political Empowerment," E. "Affirmation Meditation: The Enlightened Way to Change your Mind for Good," F. "Synchronicity: How to be in the Right Place at the Right Time"

3. **Relationships & Communication: A.** "The Secret of Successful Relationships: How to Use the Law of Attraction to Draw more Love into your Life," B. "How to Find your Soul Mate," C. "How to be at Peace with Anyone," D. "Conscious Communication," E. "Sex & Money: How to Live an Abundant, Passionate Life," F. "The Peace & Freedom Beyond Complaining"

4. **Yoga & Meditation:** A. "The Good Life & the God Life: How to be Spiritually Awakened & Materially Abundant," B. "Secrets of the Yogis: Tips for Thriving on the Spiritual Path," C. "The Bhagavad Gita and the Secret to the Meaning of Life," D. "The Gospel & the Gita: Transformation through the Teachings of Christ & Krishna," E. "Revitalize Your Body, Enlighten Your Mind, & Connect with Your Spirit," F. "Zen Teachings of Cats & Dogs"

5. **Pop Culture & Higher Consciousness:** A. "Beatles Yoga," "B. "Follow Your Yellow Brick Road: Awakening Courage, Compassion, & Inner Knowing for your Journey Home," C. *Star Wars* Yoga, The Force, & You," C1. "The Gospel of Luke (Skywalker): Jesus & the Jedis," D. "Awaken your Inner Superhero," E. "The Yoga of Oz," F. "Christ, Superman and You," G. "Rock 'n' Roll Yoga: Pop Lyrics, Higher Consciousness, & Meditation," H. "Moses, Superman and You"

6. **Creativity:** A. "Awaken your Creative Genius," B. "Walt Whitman's Enlightenment & the Awakening of your Inner Artist," C. "The Beatles, Archetypes, & You"

7. **Inner Child, Happiness, and Laughter:** A. "40 Days to a Happy Life," B. "Playing From Your Comic Mind/Playing With The Cosmic Mind," With Coach Cary Bayer & a Special Guest Appearance by God, C. "Elf Realization: Playing with your Inner Magical Child," D. "Awaken your Inner Child for the Kingdom of Heaven," (for Churches)

8. **Literature, & Religion:** A. "From Ritual to *Spi*ritual: Embodying the Teachings of Christ," B. "Rumi, Whitman, Meditation, & Enlightenment," C. "Literary Yoga: Whitman & Salinger as Writers/Seers," D. "Poetry Yoga: Whitman, the Transcendental Self, & Meditation," E. "Oy to Joy: From Kineahora to Affirmation"

9. **Seasonal:** January: A. "How to make your New Year's Resolutions Come True," May/June: B. "How to be at Peace with your Parents," November: C. "Thanksgiving, Gratitude & Prosperity," December: D. "Embrace your Inner Santa Claus: How to Embody Prosperity"

10. **Business Training for Healers:** A. "Healer, Heal Thyself: A Workshop for Counselors, Coaches, Chiropractors, Clergy, MTs, & Healers," B. "Success Aerobics: A Prosperous Mindset Creates a Successful Massage Business," C. "Build a $100,000 Massage Business in Just 1 Hour a Day," D. "How Marketing can help your Massage Business Thrive," E. "How to Communicate Effectively to Build your Massage Business," F. "How to get New Massage Clients," G. "How to Create a Successful Massage Client Referral Program," H. "How to Get more Health Care Professional Referrals," I. "How to Succeed as an MT in an Economic Slowdown," J. "How to Overcome Procrastination Now for Massage Success," K. "Massage Advertising made Easy," L. "Massage Public Relations made Easy," M. "Passive Income: An Easier Way for MTs to Prosper," N. "How the Computer & the Internet can make your Massage Business more Successful," O. "The Write Stuff: Everything you need to Know about Everything you need to Write"

11. **Stress Management:** A. "Take a Breath: An Enlightened Way to Manage Stress"

Growth Products from Cary Bayer

Books ($3 for S&H for each book)
The Prosperity Aerobics, $13
Relationships 101, $15
40 Days to a Happy Life, $16
Conscious Communication, $17
How to Overcome Procrastination Now, $20
Higher Self Meditations, $20
A Course in *Money* Miracles, $20
Breakthrough Coaching, $20
The Yoga of Entertainment: Higher Consciousness in Pop Culture, $20
"Star Wars" Yoga, the Force, & You, $20
Market and Grow a Rich Massage Business, $17
Think and Grow a Rich Massage Business, $20
Communicate and Grow a Rich Massage Business, $20
Spiritual Lampoons, $15
Trump Off the Wall (That Mexico's Gonna Pay For), $15

Ebooks ($10, except where noted, no shipping & handling)
Relationships 101, $15
The Yoga of Entertainment: Higher Consciousness in Pop Culture, $20
Awaken your Joy
Conscious Communication
Communications Breakthroughs
Affirmations Make the Heart Grow Fonder
How to Overcome Procrastination Now
Affirmations to End Procrastination

CDs ($3 for S&H for each item)
The Prosperity Aerobics Audio Book, $15
"A Prosperity Aerobics Class," A 2-cd live class from Albany, NY, $25
"Spirit and Money," A 2-cd live class from Las Vegas, NV, $25
"Conscious Communication," A 2-cd live class from Gainesville, FL, $25
"Beatles Yoga," A 2-cd live class from Newburgh, NY, $25
"Follow Your Yellow Brick Road: Awakening Courage, Compassion, & Inner Knowing for the Journey Home," A 2-cd live class from Boca Raton, FL, $25
"Magnetizing Money: Affirmations for Attracting Abundance," $15

"Affirmations make the Heart Grow Fonder," $15
"Seeds for Success: Formulas for Financial Fulfillment," $15
"How to Get New Massage Clients," A 3-cd live webinar, $35
"How to Communicate Effectively to Expand your Massage Business," A 3-cd live webinar, $35

DVDs ($3 for S&H for each item)
"The Secret of Successful Relationships: How to use the Law of Attraction to Draw more Love into your Life," A 2-hour-plus live class, from Albany, NY, $30
"How to Overcome Procrastination Now," A 2-hour live class from Albany, NY, $30
"Build a $100,000 a Year Massage Business," A 4-hour live class from NY, NY, $60
"Knowledge for Power and Success": The 1-Hour-plus Keynote Address for the 2006 American Massage Therapy Association National Convention, Atlanta, GA, $20

Mini-Books (All $10, except where noted, S&H: $2.50)

The Coaching Series
How to Discover and Live your Purpose
Awaken your Creative Genius
Follow Your Yellow Brick Road: Provisions for your Inner Journey
How to be at Peace with Anyone
Spirit and Money
Zen Teachings of Animals
Zen Teachings of Cats and Dogs

Recreation
Zen Teachings of Sports
Zen Teachings of Tennis

Consciousness & Enlightenment
Walt Whitman: Poet of Enlightenment, $12 ($3 for S&H)
Beatles Yoga, $12 ($3 for S&H)
Zen Teachings of Oz
Meditations on Christ
Proverbs from Around the World

Healer, Heal Thyself
Literary Yoga: Writers and Higher Consciousness, $12 ($3 for S&H)

Foreign Language Translations
German: Wohlstands Aerobic (translation of Prosperity Aerobics), $12
Spanish: Magnetizando el Dinero (translation of Magnetizing Money), $8

Laughter and Liberation Series
Lampoons for a New Millennium, $12 ($3 for S&H)
Laughter is the Jest Medicine: Thoughts to Laugh By
Zen in the Art of the Marx Brothers, $8
Zen in the Art of Harpo, $8

When ordering, add $2.50 per item, or $3 for books, CDs, DVDs, and longer mini-books as marked.

Make checks to: **Bayer Communications**,

1051 Hillsboro Mile, #604, Hillsboro Beach, FL 33062;
Phone: (954) 788-3380; Email: bayerpublishing@aol.com
www.carybayer.com

MAY THE FORCE BE WITH YOU!

Notes from a Future Jedi

www.ingramcontent.com/pod-product-compliance
Lightning Source LLC
Chambersburg PA
CBHW070809100426
42742CB00012B/2312